WIEL COERVER

THE REVOLUTIONARY NEW TRAINING PLAN

Foreword by
Bobby Robson

Sidgwick & Jackson
London

First published in Great Britain
in 1985 by
Sidgwick & Jackson Limited

Originally published in
The Netherlands in 1983
by Elsevier – Amsterdam
under the title
Leerplan voor de ideale voetballer

© 1983
B.V. Uitgeversmaatschappij Elsevier,
Amsterdam – The Netherlands,
Brussels – Belgium

Author of the original work:
Wiel Coerver

Text editor of the original work:
Johan Derksen

English translation:
Charles Greenwood

New text for British edition:
Mike Langley

Photographs by Robert Collette, except for those on the following pages: 22 (Sport and General); 96 (Bob Thomas); 154 (Sport and General); 176 (Central Press Photos/Photo Source); 188 (Central Press Photos/Photo Source); 194 (Bob Thomas)

Printed in Great Britain by
R. J. Acford, Industrial Estate, Chichester, Sussex
for Sidgwick & Jackson Limited
1 Tavistock Chambers, Bloomsbury Way
London WC1A 2SG

ISBN 0–283–99244–1 (cased)
ISBN 0–283–99311–1 (limp)

Foreword by Bobby Robson

During a prolonged period of forced inactivity following major heart surgery, Wiel Coerver studied video tapes of football matches and extracted from those matches outstanding examples of individual techniques. Being the student that he is, he started with a premise:

'Football is not producing technically accomplished creative players.'

It is, of course, not possible to be creative without being technically accomplished. It is also not possible to excel collectively if individual players have serious technical deficiencies. But if the premise is correct, and most of us believe that it is, why should this be and what can be done about it?

All the evidence available suggests that players now play many more matches and practise much less than used to be the case. When a young player plays 170 games in a season there is very little time left for practice! Players, of course, prefer to play rather than practise – just as a young pianist would rather play tunes than practise scales, but it is the practising of the scales which produces the technique to play the tunes correctly. So it is with football. If you are going to play better you need better techniques and the way to better techniques is to practise correctly and assiduously.

Wiel Coerver has extracted the basic techniques of all the best players in the world over the last thirty years, has established the common denominator, and has combined those techniques into a teaching programme. Given time to execute the programme the result should be players who are more accomplished technically than we have seen previously. If that objective is achieved, we shall produce more accomplished, more attractive teams.

We believe that will happen. It is for that reason that we have invited Wiel Coerver to join the coaching staff of The Football Association GM National School, where we concentrate on coaching techniques and in bringing the best potential young players into partnership with the best coaches in ideal facilities, and maximizing their time together.

Wiel Coerver is, however, much more than a student of the game of Association Football. He is a brilliant teacher and coach of the game – one of the best in the world. In a phrase, he is a master of his craft. Through this book, he has done as much as words and pictures can do, to help others achieve a similar status.

Contents

The ideal footballer

Outstanding players

Over the years the public has flocked to football grounds to see personalities such as Matthews, Di Stefano, Pelé, Eusebio, Best, Charlton, Beckenbauer, Cruyff and Maradona. They don't flock to see impersonal ball-passers.

In the 1950s the Hungarians introduced a new dimension to the game and the Brazilians were in a strong phase. For a number of years Real Madrid had football supporters on the edge of their seats, as did Ajax in their great days. But for a long time now football has produced few technically accomplished, creative players. The result is that the game has become colourless and dominated by mediocrity. Supporters look back nostalgically to the old days and increasing numbers of them stay at home.

Even at the very top level there are many players who are helpless when they are in possession of the ball because they have not mastered attacking techniques and therefore cannot make openings. A reasonable standard of football is still being played in the top clubs, of course, but this is because they spend millions to get the best players and the best coaches. These clubs disguise the real situation. In very few countries is the league championship seriously in doubt. But the general public is often not aware of the true state of affairs because only the best moments of the best games are shown on television. Even the top clubs, the ones that keep going by buying the best players, have great difficulty entertaining their fans. Lesser clubs are no longer able to manage it at all.

This is strange, though. Every year thousands of youngsters join football clubs, where they are confronted with

Diego Maradona, technically perfect

qualified trainers mass-produced in special courses. These trainers have excellent facilities and first-class material at their disposal. Because of increased leisure, the number of training hours has been doubled in recent years. Hundreds of scouts haunt the football fields, study groups are called into being, committees ponder, more and more specialized literature makes its appearance, reports are produced in abundance, and yet football does not become more attractive. More and more mediocre players and ball-passers manage to survive through effort, fitness and running ability, and this does nothing to benefit the quality of the game. There is nothing wrong with a player keeping his position through work rate, provided the game is enlivened by attractive, individual play. When the workers begin to gain the upper hand, as now, the future begins to look bleak. The public want to see more than hard work; they want the kind of brilliant individual play that gives rise to unforgettable moments.

There is a need for technical training

Quality

The personalities are disappearing, and there are also fewer and fewer goal-getters and players with ideas and creative ability. Ideas, creativity and the ability to improvise are essential to attractive football. What happens in practice is that a boy joins a club when he is eight, stops playing thirty years later as a veteran and, despite those thirty years under a qualified trainer, in nine cases out of ten he is still weak in the air, he still cannot beat a man and he is still technically limited.

If most players at the top lack the technical and creative qualities that really draw the crowds, the situation is really sad in the lower regions. In most clubs you won't find a single player who has anything of an aura or that something extra that makes the crowds sit up when he is in possession of the ball.

Training

Whereas today's players have limited technical skills, fitness and athleticism are continually on the increase. Most players keep their places because they can keep going for ninety minutes and neutralize their direct opponent. What such players lack is technical training of the kind that will mean that they are no longer helpless when they have the ball and will be able to do something more than pass it on to the next player, who cannot do anything with it either. Unfortunately, most trainers stick to unrealistic training schemes; they subject their players to all sorts of fitness tests, but nothing is done about their defective attacking techniques.

Even players who work under trainers who have been talking for years about attractive, attacking football do not receive any specialized training in

Kevin Keegan, hard work and technique

getting past opponents. Not only that, but in many cases players are not even allowed to engage in individual play during a match because it might result in loss of possession. Consequently, it is rare that any training is given in individual attacking techniques. What you see are players running over the field like members of a herd; the trainer gives yet another signal with his whistle and the players break into yet another sprint. In short, almost everywhere training sessions are impersonal and offer no scope for independence.

Unfortunately, the lack of attacking abilities means that the players use their excellent condition chiefly for defence. This in turn means that the player with the ball needs greater attacking skills than formerly if he is to create an opening or beat an opponent. The net result is that football drifts ever deeper into the doldrums.

Naturally, there is also game training: three against two, three against three, four against three, four against four, five against five, etc. These are useful positional games for players who have mastered the techniques of attack. On the other hand, over the years they have done little to improve the host of mediocre players who are helpless with the ball, particularly in difficult situations. These players should first learn the techniques needed for attack. The fact that players, particularly young players, are scarcely taught them means that, even at the end of their careers, when they get possession they are capable at most of passing the ball on or resorting to kick-and-rush football.

Training young players

Everyone is talking nowadays about training the youngsters. The evidence, however, shows that young players are growing up in an unhealthy football climate and that the people who train them, well-meaning though most of them are, are low on technical qualities. It is a tragedy for football that all these young people who are dying to learn the game have no experts they can turn to who can teach them the indispensable ball techniques. This means that they can make little progress, because there is not much to be gained by letting one eleven play against another when the players do not have ball control even without anyone to challenge them. They are seldom in possession and spend most of the game running after an opponent. Even if they had the ball more often, they would not be able to attempt anything because of their lack of mastery of the basic techniques.

Analysing training schemes for young players is often enough to bring tears to your eyes. In these decisive years the players are swamped with types of training that are useless. What can a trainer be thinking of when he makes youngsters, who want nothing better than to have a ball at their feet, run laps, jump over obstacles, do somersaults and perform other such circus tricks, or who, when a ball is finally produced, lets them wait five minutes for a turn?

There is far too little ball contact in training schemes for young players. Obviously there is not much point in them practising kicking or trapping until they have acquired a good feel for the ball, and this will only come by practising ball techniques. Once they have this they will find that a good kicking technique can be learned almost effortlessly and that they can bring the ball under control with any part of their body.

It is incredible that a lot of people still do not understand that youngsters must first devote as much energy as possible to learning the ball techniques of the game's best players, without which these players would have got nowhere. As this is virtually never done, youth training goes wrong from the very start.

Only youngsters with a natural flair, who try things despite their trainers, have a chance of becoming technically skilled footballers. Usually, however, youngsters are forbidden to engage in individual play. In the case of talented footballers it can only be hoped that they will find their way as quickly as possible into a big club, where they can learn a lot from older players. The pity of it is that many youngsters stop after a time because they make too little technical progress and therefore cease to enjoy the game. The rest remain mediocre, because they continue to receive too little technical training throughout their career.

Technical training

Every trainer in a specialized sport knows that technical training is a question of constant repetition until a particular technique has been completely mastered. The only people who appear not to understand this are most football trainers, who attend courses which are dominated by physiology.

In almost all sports, learners, and particularly young learners, practise under trainers who can demonstrate to perfection what they have to learn, and keep on doing so until such time as they have mastered the techniques in question.

This is the case even in sports in which there is no opponent whose job it is to thwart the attempt to carry out the technique. It is scarcely ever the case, however, in football, even though no other sport is as many-sided or requires such a wide range of techniques if it is to be played attractively. This is a further reason for concluding that footballers are trained wrongly from the very beginning.

Yet another indication that something is amiss is the fact that one never sees youngsters practising on their own outside the normal training sessions. The fields that were once put to such intensive use are becoming emptier and emptier. Where do you see boys playing football nowadays? If the trainers of our young players do not make them practise the techniques during the club sessions it is not surprising that the present generation have no mastery of feinting or anything else needed to beat an opponent. Trainers should not only practise the techniques during club sessions; they should give young players homework. As this is almost never done, it never occurs to most players to work on their own.

Individual play

Top footballers can excel collectively only thanks to their individual qualities. All of them owe their class to the fact that they can engage in individual play at the right moment. There are dozens of occasions in a game when individual initiative is needed for the collective cause. It is always the footballers who are capable of individual play who decide matches and thrill the crowds. Such players give colour to the game. Without their individual qualities they would be no different from the mass of players just below the very top.

Unfortunately, in training, boys with flair are not allowed to indulge in individual play, while boys without it are simply left to their fate without being taught the essential techniques at the club sessions. On the other hand, they

Individual
play is forbidden

George Best, a star thanks to his individual qualities

Michel Platini, ability to beat a man

are required to play collective football, which is unreasonable, because they cannot control the ball even without an opponent, let alone with one. As soon as they find themselves in a difficult situation all they can do is pass the ball on to another player or belt it upfield. The football that this produces does not bear watching.

In the decisive years of their careers young players spend most of their time running after opponents, because helping in defence is apparently very important. It is very simple to make life impossible for an opponent who cannot do very much with the ball anyway.

Players who are not trained to undertake personal initiatives will always remain dull footballers. If youngsters were to devote all their energies to perfecting individual play, we would see much better football in the future.

Trainers

There are various categories of trainers and trainer-coaches, but there are very few who can teach a player the essential techniques. Which category is responsible for the separate components of the game is not clear. Most players

who have come across all categories in the course of their careers still have limited technical capabilities when they retire.

Teachers at a school or professors at a university determine what their pupils or students will be taught. The quality of a university stands or falls on the expertise of its professors.

The same applies in the world of football. How players develop depends on the quantity and quality of what they are taught to practise. This is not an attack on trainer-coaches. Every one of them has the interests of football at

Bobby Robson, practical coach

heart, but unfortunately, because their training as players and as coaches was deficient, they are not capable of teaching their players the countless ball techniques of the world's best footballers, of inspiring them and convincing them of the value of practising for themselves outside the official sessions.

Coaches

The absence of sound technical training for footballers means that there are scarcely any good coaches. This does not in its turn mean that there are no good managers, because there certainly are. Most of them work for the top clubs, the clubs that buy the best players. They do not train the players with whom they work. The manager's job is to create a good football climate and mould a strong team out of the players available. In the course of their careers players of the likes of Pelé, Di Stefano, Happel, Beckenbauer and Cruyff have used their superior techniques to solve countless difficult problems on the field, and in doing so have become football personalities. Because of this they have the feeling for the game which the good coach or manager needs and which cannot be acquired by any kind of theoretical training. They don't talk twaddle about tactical concepts; whatever they say makes football sense. They know their job and they have strong personalities. Football stands in such need of these winners that they can take their pick of the best clubs.

What they cannot do, however, is turn mediocre players into stars. Their training sessions are mostly of a practical kind, a lot of games and positional play in which the good footballers can exhibit their tactical and technical qualities. Most of the players, how-

Teachers
lack practical experience

Ernst Happel, formerly top player, now top coach

that footballers must be brought up in accordance with their courses and they also decide who is fit to be a trainer or coach and who is not. Even top players, who for years have demonstrated their understanding of the game and given immeasurable pleasure to the public, are dependent on the teachers and their courses. The teachers too have the interests of the game at heart, but unfortunately most of them, and most of the people who design the courses, have far too little practical experience.

Anyone who does not know what it feels like to beat an opponent, to see a solo run capped with success, or to be able to do more or less anything with the ball, automatically lacks specific qualities needed to train footballers. Anyone who has not spent years on the field turning difficult situations to his team's advantage through his technical qualities and tactical skills lacks the practical experience required to make a good coach. These teachers could do with a good dose of self-criticism. Self-criticism is needed in any kind of job, and certainly in theirs. Not for a moment does it occur to them that there might be something wrong with their courses. They don't even ask themselves whether their pupils ought not to be capable of teaching footballers the various ball techniques individually before they get their diplomas. The teachers have thought of every conceivable way of keeping their pupils busy for years; only the most important thing, teaching the techniques of the best players, has been omitted from the list of examinations. What I should like to know is, if qualified trainers cannot teach footballers these techniques, who can?

ever, do not have these qualities, and there is nothing even the best coaches can do about it. They lack the practice material, the patience and the gift of getting players to master the techniques. Being naturally talented they cannot identify with players who must reach the top through intensive and well-directed training.

None the less, football owes a lot to managers. Over the years they have taken many a club to the top and given the fans a lot of pleasure. Without them football would really be in a bad way. Fortunately it never used to be necessary – and still isn't in some countries – for a manager to take all sorts of theoretical courses, otherwise these top men might have been lost to football.

Teachers

Though the quality of the game is showing no signs of benefiting from the fact that every club has one or more trainers with years of study behind them, the teachers continue to insist

Courses

The situation as regards courses in the different countries is chaotic. If you compare all the courses the only conclusion you can come to is that there is not even agreement on how a trainer-coach should teach footballers. In one country you have to study for five years before you're allowed to train top players; in another all you need is to take a one-month course; while there are still countries in which you require no formal qualifications at all. In practice, one finds that the best football is by no means played in the country with the longest course; in fact, the best technical football is played in the countries with short courses. In no other profession are there such incredible differences in qualifications. The courses do not differ only in duration; they also differ widely in content. But they all tend to be dependent and impersonal, particularly in the countries where you have to study for years before you can call yourself a trainer.

This is strange in a sport that requires so much technical creativity, nerve and self-confidence. Teaching footballers to dominate the ball and their opponent is far more important than all the theories, concepts, tests, physiology, anatomy and knowledge of statutes and rules put together. The trainers are taught all about physiology and anatomy and then go on to make the players do the same exercises irrespective of differences in musculature and constitution. Obviously, a basic knowledge of how the body functions is worth having, but you must also learn how to apply it. This can be done in a very simple and comprehensive way without spending years on it. Only fools preach scholarly sermons on football. It is a mistake to subject people, particularly ex-footballers who have worked for years under good coaches, to this sort of thing for too long.

The advantage of short courses for former players is that they won't be lost to football and can show straightaway whether they are suited to being trainer-coaches.

Literature

There is no agreement either in the specialist literature on how footballers ought to be trained. Everyone has his own ideas, theories and methods. Again, most practice books are written by people who are not inhibited by actual experience. The majority of books contain long lists of unrealistic exercises.

In Hungary the books are written by teachers in sport academies and schools for trainers. All levels of effort have been scientifically tested, which is certainly interesting, but nowhere can readers discover how to learn the techniques of outstanding Hungarians such as Puscas, Hidegkuti, Bozsik and Kocsis, who were playing the best football in the world in the 1950s

Technical training

Personalities
are becoming rare

The German books are full of gymnastic exercises and pedantic texts written with an entirely misplaced arrogance. The English books are attractive to look at, but coaching amounts to very little in England and this is reflected perfectly in the practice books.

Naturally, books are occasionally published which have something sensible to say, but in none of them can you find out how to learn the techniques essential to making the most out of ball possession.

Personality

For a footballer to play attractive football and be capable of making the best use of a wide range of situations he must have wide-ranging technical abilities, a thorough understanding of the game and personality. It is obvious that if those rare footballers who are capable of individual play are forbidden to engage in it and games are thereby deprived of their highlights, the result will be totally unattractive to the public.

As players do not work on their own – even full-time professionals will hang around for hours at a time without showing the least initiative, even though they have time enough to work on their technical deficiencies – the initiative will have to come from the trainers. Only when coaches teach them the right ball techniques can players develop into personalities, because most situations that arise in a game demand independence, self-confidence and character.

In no other sport does a player have so many possibilities when he is in possession. Unfortunately, the majority of players are forced to take the easiest course and pass the ball on. The result is that spectators are being

Franz Beckenbauer, personality

systematically driven from the stands. Instead of players being taught to play courageous attacking football, fear of failure predominates. Naturally, a personality requires not only technical skills but also tactical, mental and moral qualities to match.

Tactics

Not only do the best players show us how youngsters should be trained; they also show us how footballers develop tactically. If at a young age you already have the ball techniques to make decisive plays, your tactical development is automatic. The big problem in football today is that all the players who unfailingly get rid of the ball to a team-mate stagnate tactically. Moreover, almost all of the technically limited players are in excellent condition and use it solely for defensive tactics, the reason being that attacking tactics require a mastery of attacking ball techniques. Coaches preach endless tactical sermons to players and the future trainers who attend the courses have to make match analyses, but talking about tactics is pointless if players do not have the techniques needed in attack.

If a coach wants a team to play defensively there is no problem at all, because football literature is crammed with defensive tactics. No tactical concepts exist which make it possible for technically limited footballers to create openings against a defence that is superior in number. There is no point in letting players with limited technical skills touch the ball only once or twice in training sessions when they cannot even control it without the presence of an opponent. The only people who can develop tactically are technically gifted players, because their technical skills mean that they

Johan Cruyff, leadership on the field

Young players
waste energy in training sessions

constantly encounter and find solutions for new situations. As they can do nothing with the ball when they have it, technically weak players will also remain tactically weak throughout their career.

Intelligence

Because of the chaotic situation as regards courses for trainers and coaches, nothing is done to develop intelligence in footballers. As there is rarely any individual training, it is difficult for players to think about and discuss their shortcomings and progress. They wait for the trainer to blow his whistle and all of them go through the same routine despite their totally different positions in the team. The result is that lack of interest and indifference have crept in. Players do not really have any thoughts about their own development, which is odd considering that young people in all sections of society have become more conscious and more independent. What young people want is to be convinced of the meaningfulness of what they are doing, but there is as yet no trace of this in football.

The trainer tells the players what to do in the training sessions and they do it like faithful retainers. They are all given their assignments before a game and dance unquestioningly to the trainer's tune, even if it means running after a shirt number for ninety minutes. Inevitably, players have scarcely made any progress when they come to the end of their careers. They do not open their mouths even when a game is being discussed. They are only heard when they are criticized, and then they know precisely what other players have done wrong.

Self-evaluation is completely ignored in training footballers. They can talk for hours about games that have been played but you seldom hear them talking about the training sessions that determine their technical development. This is because there is little logic in the sessions and they are never discussed. You can't really blame the players when coaches do not know how to improve a footballer's technical skills. The consequence is that none of the players know how they can work on their technical shortcomings individually.

Inner stimulation

Inappropriate exercises and the failure to concentrate on technical shortcomings result in inadequate technical and tactical development, but the resultant lack of success also means that nothing is stimulated inside the players. It is incomprehensible that so little is done to give young players a broad technical base; it is even more so that so little is done as regards the inner development of the players, because under expert coaching it is precisely these inner forces which determine a player's performance. State of mind plays an important part in football. Forces can be called upon that are seldom put to use. Just like intelligence and physical powers, however, these inner forces have to be developed. A player's state of mind can have a positive influence on his performances, and success produces a particularly agreeable feeling in young people. Unfortunately, players who are not taught in the right way will never know that feeling; youngsters cannot achieve success if they waste the greater part of their energy running and doing other unsuitable exercises, with no motivation to train with a ball.

There is nothing easier or more gratifying than training young footballers if you can really teach. Young people are not lazy. On the contrary, they are thirsty for activity and stimulation, and more than willing to learn. This is what makes it so sad that they are seldom given anything sensible to practise, to which they can devote themselves heart and soul. They do not drop by the wayside through weakness but because they don't make the technical progress necessary for success. Their ambition, inspiration and dedication are undermined and they drop out. Usually they then find themselves in even less satisfactory sur-

Zico, technician

roundings, with the result that many of them are lost to football for ever.

Morale

A footballer can have the proper morale, radiate self-assurance and nerve, only if he has mastered his techniques. Self-assurance is impossible as long as there is a part of his game that he has not mastered. For this reason, a weak, dependent player, a ball-passer, can never have the proper match mentality. Unfortunately, there are players of this kind in every team.

Only the outstanding players have the required morale. They have a tremendous match mentality, because they have mastered every facet of the game; there can be no surprises for them.

Levels of physical condition are constantly being raised but they are being devoted to defensive tactics, with the result that fewer and fewer players with morale are to be seen on football fields. Almost all the players one sees are uncertain when they have the ball. Developing morale in players requires success obtained by proper training in attacking techniques.

Criticism

During his training a footballer is of course taught useful things. The point is that technical creativity, the thing that draws the crowds, is shamefully neglected and, because of this, football is in difficulties.

Fortunately for the game, little more can be done to improve the defensive qualities and condition of professional footballers. After all, a team can only use eleven men in defence. Hopefully trainers will come to see that for years now their approach has been too one-sided. Most of their training books can be thrown into the dustbin, because all those tests and all that circuit and condition training are no longer what is needed. If we want to resuscitate football and make it attractive again for players and public alike we must devote all our energies to teaching the techniques of the best players. That this is the only aspect of football on which no books have yet been written is in itself sufficient justification for criticizing the present approach to training.

Willem van Hanegem, match mentality

Techniques of top footballers

Training plan

Only the very best footballers are still capable of exhilarating the public. The plan presented here is geared to the specific qualities of those players. It makes it possible to deliberately set out to become a player with abilities far above the average. In the beginning you will devote all your energies to becoming at least as gifted individually as the recognized top players. You then go on to apply these techniques in practice and competitive forms, group games and matches, which will also develop your tactical skills.

The plan contains all the qualities you need. It is intended for footballers who want to master as many techniques as possible and have the mentality to do so. Boys who start on this training plan at the age of ten will have the technical ability of a top footballer by the time they are sixteen. They can then apply these techniques individually and collectively. To achieve this as quickly and as efficiently as possible the training plan has been divided up into phases and each phase into technical components. Specific training is undertaken for each component.

The innumerable ball contacts in the first phase ensure that you learn to control the ball and your body. This control will become increasingly perfected as you progress through the plan.

In the second phase you put these ball techniques to work. You learn to keep possession of the ball despite the presence of an opponent, to shield it and to come away with it.

In the third phase you learn to get past an opponent on your own or with the help of a team-mate. You then practise through passes, which will cause problems for any defence.

Pelé, superior technique

The fourth phase is concerned with learning to shoot, head and finish off individual moves. The techniques that have been learned are then used in group games in which the emphasis is on scoring.

In the fifth phase it becomes clear that in working on the techniques you automatically acquire optimal match condition.

Not until the sixth phase, when all the attacking techniques have been mastered, is attention paid to defensive qualities. Once all the techniques have been mastered and you can apply them at speed and against full opposition, you move on to the last phase.

In this seventh phase the emphasis is on moving without the ball. The object is to ensure that throughout a game you will be in the right place at the right time.

Naturally, players of sixteen and over, for whom competition is important, do not need to adhere precisely to this order. They can decide the possibilities and variations for themselves, based on which of the techniques they have already mastered. Trainers can construct a programme from the components in the different phases in accordance with their wishes as regards emphasis. There are, of course, many more types of practice than are given in this book. Trainers can use their improvisational and creative abilities to elaborate on the various components.

The main objective of this training plan is to ensure that young players will devote themselves heart and soul to learning the attacking techniques of the best footballers. Older players who missed such training in their youth can use the plan to improve their attacking qualities.

Trainer/coach

To apply this training plan to all those who want to become technically creative players, coaches are needed who have mastered its contents and can demonstrate them to perfection. This will not be all that easy in the beginning, but every player who has command of all the techniques is itching to pass on his knowledge.

If you yourself have had to work really hard to learn all the techniques it is easier to convince others of the purpose of the exercises. Former top players often have trouble as coaches because they themselves usually drew on natural talents and find it difficult to identify with players who have to work really hard at it. For this reason they often make better managers.

The great strength of trainer-coaches who have had to go through it all themselves lies in their patience and ability to inspire. They have no trouble at all in encouraging less gifted players and convincing them that they too can learn all the techniques.

In teaching his players the attacking qualities of the top footballers the coach will be doing exactly what is needed and all other types of training become superfluous. They merely create confusion.

The only other thing that is needed is a manager, a winner, to work on the team as a whole. The coach ensures that the individual players receive a technical training that is many-sided and creative; the manager turns them into a team. Obviously, the two things cannot be entirely separated, because the coach also works on collective aspects of the training sessions, while the manager will do everything possible to make his players even better individually. The main objective of the coach, though, is to produce as many technically creative players as possible, whereas that of the manager is to mould these players into a team.

Producing trainers

As many trainers as possible must be produced who are capable of implementing this training plan, especially among young players, in order to raise the level of technical creativity. The good coaches will emerge from this new group of trainers of their own accord.

It is clear that the future of football depends on these trainer-coaches. They must teach all the attacking techniques to all those players who do not have a natural gift for them so that football can once again become an attractive spectator sport.

Young players

The very young should not be troubled with planned training and assignments. Let them carry on as they are and they will unconsciously be learning how to cope with the ball. There is no point in team play, because they are only interested in the ball and the goal. Rather than real matches they should

Young players long for technical training

play group games. In this way they will touch the ball a lot, whereas in a real game, eleven a side, their contact with the ball would be sporadic.

Proper training should begin at ten years of age. If young tennis players, gymnasts and swimmers can happily train for a few hours a day to attain something in their sport, young footballers can easily practise the ball techniques, feints and other movements for hours, because they are not very strenuous. The trainers must convince them of the importance of also

training with the ball outside the club sessions. They will not take much persuading and the result will be that they will be in almost constant contact with the ball for at least eight hours a week, which is more than the average junior player manages in a year.

Trainers should always give brief explanations of the exercises, demonstrate them properly and then correct their pupils. There is no point yet in organizing big games. In small games they will have possession much more often and try out all the techniques

Training the new generation

they have learned. In these training sessions it is essential that players carry out one of the techniques they have been taught before passing the ball.

During adolescence even more attention must be paid to co-ordination in possession. The players must not carry out the exercises in a cramped fashion; the emphasis should always be on suppleness. When the players have attained reasonable proficiency in most techniques they must start to take initiatives in group games. They must be made to realize that if they are to achieve their aims they must not waste energy on pointless running. They must make as many individual and creative moves as possible. These foster flair and self-confidence. From the age of thirteen onwards the training must not only be technically creative; it must also be dynamic and explosive. At the same time, the finishing touches are added as regards perfecting techniques. Up to the age of sixteen players have all the time they need to learn all the techniques and apply them in game situations. This is much more important than winning a match. In recent years, much too often the choice has fallen on physically strong, fit boys who still belong to the ranks of the mediocre ten years later because they have not received a sound technical training.

Technical development

In the initial phase all training should be technical. Only sprinting speed is largely inherited; all the other abilities can be acquired, though years of the right kind of training are needed.

The first component of phase one, the basic techniques, gives rise to the most problems because proper co-ordination has to be acquired. This is something that comes easier to some players than to others. The players who have difficulty with it must be helped and encouraged by the trainer, because otherwise they will fall by the wayside or remain technically mediocre.

Though top footballers demonstrate their perfect movements regularly, young players often fail to learn from what they see. After the demonstration they are simply left gaping. A single demonstration is not enough to master such techniques; it requires very intensive training. If the club sessions are not enough, naturally extra training will be needed at home. As soon as the players begin to have some success they will do more on their own.

Any footballer can learn all the techniques, but it will cost a senior more time than a junior. It is easier to learn a new movement than to improve one that you have learned incorrectly. Experience shows that a player with a wide range of ball techniques finds it significantly easier to learn new movements and also enjoys doing so.

The different techniques recur so frequently in this training plan that sufficient perfection is developed after a time that it is no longer possible to discern whether it is an acquired or a natural movement. As soon as a player has a perfect command of the techniques he goes on to try them out against opposition. All the components are dealt with in the first four phases of the plan. Thereafter the techniques must be applied in practice and competitive games, but there is little point in such games until the players have mastered the techniques.

The basis of this plan is the broadest possible individual technical training, which is essential if footballers are to play well collectively.

Football personality

Using this method, training is based on the plan; players no longer have to wait for the trainer's whistle, they can also practise the different techniques independently. This will give rise to a new generation of footballers who do not leave everything to the trainer but think about, talk about and work at developing their own potentialities.

Players who choose the easiest course in training sessions, passing the

Karl-Heinz Rummenigge, technique at speed

ball on, will do the same thing in matches. There is no room any more for players like that. The techniques that have been learned must be applied; the coach must demand individual play, there have to be one-two combinations and the ball must continually be played to team-mates running between or around defenders. Dependence and lack of personality are taboo.

Football personalities reveal themselves as such in difficult situations; they make decisive moves. Trainers,

Paulo Rossi, top scorer

therefore, must demand of young players that they make use of possession every time with the help of the techniques they have learned and that they make as many decisive moves as possible.

Tactical development

If a technically perfect footballer is weak tactically he will still be helpless in most situations. Choosing the correct tactical solution, making a fast move at the right moment and being in

the right position to receive the ball at the right time are not things that can be learned through theory.

In this training plan the players are given the opportunity to develop tactically. They first learn the techniques, at speed and looking beyond the ball. They then learn to make the best use of the ball every time they are in possession. Only then can they develop tactical skills, both with and without the ball. However, a player's tactical development is unpredictable. As trainer, you are in complete control as regards technical development, but experience shows that a player's tactical development does not always match his technical development.

Development of intelligence

Anyone who trains in accordance with this plan knows exactly what he is doing. He is learning the techniques of the best footballers. He is no longer engaged in unrealistic exercises which jump from one thing to another. Every component is gone through systematically and the player knows precisely what its purpose is. As he soon begins to see results he will enjoy it more and more. The coach should regularly discuss progress with the group and with the individual players, and the players should automatically take part in the discussion. Just as at school, the player will know exactly where he is, which is essential if irritation and frustration are to be avoided. Healthy development requires that the player should do his share of the thinking and talking and should be capable of self-criticism, things which have thus far received far too little attention.

Players must think and talk about training sessions and matches for the simple reason that when a game is in

progress one player has a lot more influence than ten coaches.

Emotional development

Training requires inspiration and animation. These inner driving forces determine both how fast a player develops and what level he reaches. Optimal use must therefore be made of the vitality of the young and they must be given a sufficient taste of success so that they become involved heart and soul. Technically creative action gives any footballer a wonderful feeling and is highly stimulating. It works as a kind of drug, calling forth ever more vital powers. Football is, above everything, passion and emotion. That is why a healthy football climate is so important for a young player.

Developing morale

All top footballers have flair, a match mentality, self-confidence, nerve and high morale. They have acquired these things through their natural abilities. This training plan makes it possible for any footballer to acquire the same kind of morale by learning all the techniques of the top players. Thus equipped, any footballer can become an attractive footballer.

Coaches must make sure that there is a healthy football climate in which there is no room for monotonous training sessions, laxity and drab routine. A player never stops growing. He can never learn everything in the technical sphere, his grasp of the game can never be perfect and the possibilities for solving match situations are so numerous that ten books could be written about them with ease. Most trainers and players do not even know that there is such a thing as inner forces in football. It is a fact, none the less, that

Anyone can become a good footballer

Anyone can become a good footballer

ever greater morale is needed in a player if he is to break through the wall of highly fit defenders. Players must continue to work on in the full awareness of what they are doing. There is so much to specialize in and perfect that no such animal as the complete footballer has ever been produced or will ever be produced, any more than the complete trainer or coach will ever be produced, let alone the complete training plan.

This training plan, however, demonstrates that any normally gifted footballer with ambition and the right mentality can learn the techniques of the top footballers. With these, he will get much more pleasure and satisfaction out of his career and football will finally become attractive to the public again.

Peter Shilton
Technique personified

Peter Shilton is technique personified and there isn't a goalkeeper in the world who cannot learn from him about marshalling defences and about leaving nothing to chance.

For example, Shilton practises punching with either fist, explaining: 'If I had a favoured punching arm, opponents would quickly learn to block it.'

This book's study of individual techniques began through working with goalkeepers in Holland, particularly Jan van Beveren of Sparta Rotterdam, during the sixties. Shilton, then a boy in Leicester, was arriving at similar conclusions himself and he has now broken down goalkeeping into these five components:

physical presence

agility

bravery

good hands and

concentration.

The level of concentration is shown by Shilton's thoughts as an opponent shoots:
'I think of his body position, his angle, how hard he'll hit it, my own position. Will he clip it, bend it, drive it high or low?
'All that runs through my mind in the time the ball takes to leave the boot.'

Phase 1

Controlling body and ball

1. *Basic techniques*

2. *Suppleness and agility on the ball*

3. *Fast footwork on the ball*

4. *Looking beyond the ball*

5. *Feinting*

6. *Creating and improvising*

7. *Kicking and trapping*

The purpose of the first phase is to learn as much control as possible over body and ball. It is not the intention to demonstrate by means of a host of techniques that there is too little training with the ball in football. It would be easy to fill a whole book merely with exercises on the ball. You will soon find that out for yourself when you begin to train intensively with the ball and discover that you are enjoying it more and more. Success acts like a drug; as soon as you begin to feel you are making progress you want to train even more with the ball, thereby increasing your skill. There is no other sport in which you need so much technique as in football. You are constantly confronted with different situations, added to which you have one or more opponents to cope with. Good technique is essential for dealing confidently with all the different situations which arise in the course of a game.

The techniques needed for you to become as strong as possible on the ball are divided into five categories, four of which are dealt with in this first phase. The fifth category, getting past an opponent, is dealt with in phase three. Of the various techniques given here, those that suit a particular player best and prove the most successful will be the ones he will shortly apply in practice.

The emphasis in the second section is on acquiring the necessary suppleness on the ball. The third

section is concerned with fast footwork, speeding up the rhythm of the legs. At the end of each component the player goes through all the exercises combined in whatever way he wishes.

The trainer must get the players to learn these techniques by constantly repeating each exercise, if necessary through individual training sessions, and they must be given exercises to do as homework, because all of them can be practised in a small amount of space. Despite the fact that the players have not yet properly mastered the techniques, the training sessions must always be closed or interrupted by a game. This adds to the attractiveness of the sessions. The emphasis in such games must be on the exercises that have been dealt with. The players must be compelled to use the techniques they have learned. As the players are continually dribbling in these sessions this important component does not need to be dealt with. By the time he comes to the end of phase one a player has sufficient control over his body and the ball that he is no longer helpless when he is in possession. He can now go on to develop into a technically skilled, creative footballer.

1. Basic techniques

Pivot the ball across the body with the inside of the right foot, then play it forward with the outside of the left foot. Pivot it across the body with the inside of the left foot, and so on

In the same way that a pupil at school cannot progress with his studies until he has learned to read and write, a footballer cannot play or train effectively if he has not mastered the basic techniques. The basic techniques are used in changing direction, swivelling and turning, but also in shielding the ball, correcting and coming away with it when there is no one in a position

Practising the basic movements in a zigzag pattern

Pivot the ball under the body with the inside of the instep, play it forward with the inside of the other foot, then repeat

Pivot the ball with the outside of the foot, play it forward with the inside of the foot, pivot it with the outside of the foot, and so on

Basic
techniques

Pivot the ball with the inside of the instep, play it forward with the outside of the same foot, then pivot it with the outside of the foot and play it forward with the inside of the same foot

to receive a pass. In situations like this the best footballers use one or more of these techniques to create an opening or a better situation for a pass.

The basic techniques can be practised in various forms, individually or in twos, in the latter case with one player always resting. They can be practised in an open space, over the length of the

Practising the basic movements back and forth

Place the outside of the foot behind the ball, turn on your own axis and play the ball with the outside of the foot

Place the inside of the foot behind the ball, turn on your own axis and play the ball with the inside of the foot

Basic techniques

Play the ball across the body with the toe of the boot, then play it forward with the outside of the other foot. Play it back across the body with this foot using the toe of the boot, etc.

field, zigzag, in a circle, in a triangle, in a square or in free arrangements.

As little dribbling as possible is done between the exercises in order to devote as much time as possible and all the energy to acquiring these techniques. Tempo is adapted to the players' skill.

Turn the ball under the body with the toe of the boot and play it forward with the inside of the other foot

Practising the basic movements at random

Step over the ball with the inside of the foot, then play the ball forward with the inside of the other foot. Do the same thing starting with this foot

Basic techniques

Stop the ball, place the same foot behind the ball by means of a quick turn and take the ball in the opposite direction

Practising the basic movements in turns, zigzag, back and forth, in a small triangle and at random

Trap the ball under the foot, turn quickly and play the ball with the other foot

Place the leg supporting the weight of the body next to the ball, then play the ball behind the supporting leg with the inside of the other foot

Basic techniques

Draw the ball towards you under your foot and play it forward again with the outside of the same foot, then do the same thing with the other foot

Practising the basic movements in threes, with two balls, always with one player resting

Draw the ball back under the foot, stop it with the inside of the same foot and play it forward with the inside of the other foot

Supporting leg next to the ball, draw the ball under the body and play it across the back of the supporting leg with the inside of the foot

In a circle, working towards a cone and then away from it. All the exercises can also be carried out in a small triangle, zigzag or in a free arrangement

Practising zigzag from cone to cone, up on the right, down on the left

Basic
techniques

A row of cones, with the players practising once at a cone and then once in free space, then once at a cone again, etc.

Each player practises the basic techniques in his own triangle

Practising zigzag in a circle

Practising in threes with two balls. The two with a ball can practise as they wish and are relieved in turn by the third player

Practising in twos with two balls, back and forth

Basic techniques

Zigzag arrangement. The player at the back works forward, carrying out a basic movement when he reaches each player. When he gets to the front he takes up position in the zigzag arrangement

Threes with two balls. Two players practise the basic techniques together and are relieved in turn by the player who is resting

Twos with one ball in a circle. One of the pair rests while the other works between two players

Twos with one ball in a circle. One of the pair rests while the other works between the cone in the middle and his partner

Four pairs working in two triangles. In each triangle, two players practise while the other two rest. If the centre cone is taken away the four pairs can work around a square

Basic
techniques

Twos with one ball in a zigzag arrangement. One rests while the other practises between two players. This exercise can, of course, also be practised in a small triangle, back and forth or freely

Right: Twos in a row. One rests while the other practises between two players

Twos with one ball. Two players in turn carry out the exercises on each side of the cones

Above: Fours with two balls. The two with a ball practise on each side of the two resting players. The exercises are always carried out with the outside foot

Left: Twos with one ball in a square. The exercises can be practised freely, in a small triangle in front of the player's partner, between two players or around the square

Basic
techniques

*Twos with one ball in a free arrange-
ment. The players with a ball practise
the techniques as they wish*

*Twos with one ball in a circle. The one
with the ball practises between two
players*

*Twos with one ball. The players work
around the triangle, between two players or freely*

Two groups of three with one ball each. One player from each group sets off with the ball at speed. When he reaches the other group he carries out a movement and plays the ball back to his own group. He then joins the other group

Threes with one ball. The player with the ball practises between the two other players, each player practising in turn.

Two groups of three, each with one ball. One player from each group sets off with the ball at speed. When he reaches the other group he executes a movement, goes back to the middle, where he executes another movement, then back to the other group again, where he executes a third movement before playing the ball back to his own group and joining the other group

Basic
techniques

Three groups of three, each with one ball, in a triangle. One player from each group sets off with the ball at speed towards the next group. When he reaches it he executes a movement, plays the ball back to his own group and joins the group where he is

Two players at the back set off, execute a movement when they reach the front players, come back, execute another movement when they reach the back players and then take up position at the front

Below: threes with one ball. Players take turns to engage in free practice, executing movements when they come to the cones and fellow players

2. Suppleness and agility on the ball

In carrying out all the basic techniques, concentrate on suppleness and agility. With the inside of the foot pivot the ball to the inside of the other foot, the knees almost touching the ball

Draw the ball across the body with the toe of the boot. Bending the knees deeply, play the ball forward with the outside of the other foot

Trap the ball; move the leg sideways as far as possible and play the ball with the outside of the other foot. Trap it, etc.

That scarcely any attention is paid to suppleness and agility on the ball can be seen from the angular and uneconomical movements characteristic of European players. Players who excel in these things, such as the Brazilians, were born with them; they did not acquire them through special training. The need for special training is evinced by the woodenness with which young players move, because it has become clear by now that all those gymnastic exercises do not increase suppleness and agility on the ball. This can only be achieved through appropriate exercises with the ball.

A start has already been made with the basic techniques. These involve total movements in which both the ankle and the hip joints are used, while the spine gets a lot of exercise in all the quick turns that have to be made. All of the basic techniques can be used for the purpose of acquiring suppleness and agility on the ball, but the body must now be kept as close to the ground as possible by bending the knees deeply, and in changes of direction the supporting leg must be as far away from the ball as possible in order to keep the body low.

A player who has suppleness and agility on the ball is more attractive to watch and it costs him less energy to execute moves, whether in training sessions or in a game.

Suppleness and agility on the ball

Draw the ball back with the sole of the boot, then play it forward with the outside of the same foot

Practising the basic techniques individually with the emphasis on suppleness and agility

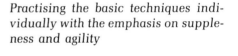

Draw the ball back with the sole of the boot, then turn it away with the outside of the same foot. Draw the ball back again, etc.

Combination of the previous exercises. Draw the ball back with the sole and play it forward with the outside, draw it back with the sole and turn it away with the outside

Suppleness and agility on the ball

Roll the ball with the inside of the foot, trap it with the inside of the other foot, tap it and roll it with the inside of the other foot

Practising the basic movements with the emphasis on suppleness and agility

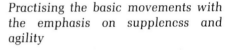

Roll the ball with the inside of the foot, trap it with the inside of the other foot and again roll it in a forward direction

Roll the ball with the outside of the foot, play it forward with the outside of the other foot, then roll it with the outside of that foot

Suppleness and agility on the ball

Roll the ball under the body with the outside of the foot, stop the ball with the same foot and roll it with the outside of the other foot

Practising the basic techniques in twos with the emphasis on suppleness and agility

Flick the ball up with the outside of the foot

Playing the ball forward with the outside of each foot alternately in a zigzag pattern

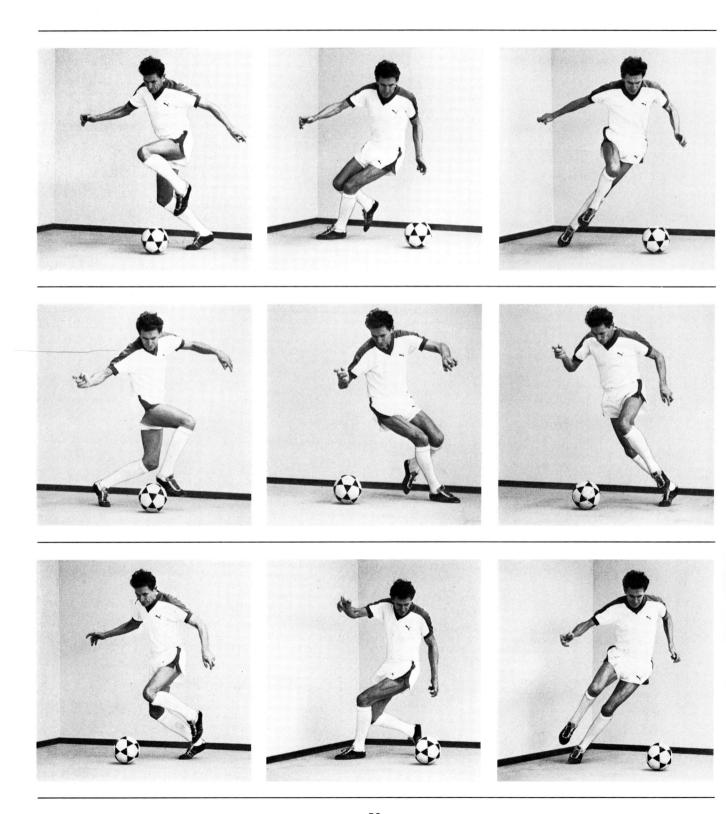

Suppleness and agility on the ball

Step over the ball with the inside of the right foot. Play the ball forward with the inside of the left foot and immediately set off with it. Stop the ball and repeat the exercise in a forward direction

The same exercise but using the right and left foot alternately, moving back and forth on the spot

Practising in turns in pairs with the emphasis on suppleness and agility

Step over the ball with the inside of the foot, play it forward with the inside of the other foot while twisting, again step over the ball with the inside of the foot, and so on

Suppleness and agility on the ball

What you see on these pages are merely some examples, because the emphasis is on suppleness and agility in all the forms in which the basic techniques are practised

3. Fast footwork on the ball

Tap the ball under the body from one foot to the other in a zigzag pattern

Pivot the ball with the inside of the instep to the inside of the other foot. Give it a couple of quick taps and pivot it with the inside of the instep of the other foot

Play the ball under the body to the inside of the other foot with the toe of the boot. Give it a couple of quick taps and then play it under the body with the toe of the other boot

Trainers pay little attention to speed of footwork on the ball even though players are given less and less room. The speed with which a player acts when he is in possession is often of decisive importance, particularly in the opposing team's penalty area. These techniques are also needed to dodge tackles by defenders. Again, use can be made here of the basic techniques, but now the contact of the feet with the ball must be as fast and supple as possible. After each exercise the ball is tapped quickly to the other foot and the exercise repeated with this foot. This means that a player touches the ball thousands of times an hour, which in addition to improving his rhythm of movement and speed of footwork also develops feel for the ball in both legs. All players greatly enjoy these exercises, which can be carried out in a small amount of space.

Fast footwork
on the ball

Roll the ball under the foot, give it a couple of taps and roll it under the other foot

Tap the ball with the bottom of the foot to the inside of the other foot, give it a couple of intermediate taps, then tap it back with the bottom of the foot to the inside of the first foot

Draw the ball back under the sole of the boot and play it forward with the outside of the same foot. After a couple of intermediate taps, draw the ball back with the other foot

Practising fast footwork

Fast footwork
on the ball

Draw the ball back to the inside of the same foot, tap it a couple of times and then draw it back with the other foot to the inside of that foot

Practising fast footwork in a free space

Draw the ball back under the boot and play it forward or sideways with the outside of the same foot. Give it a couple of taps and repeat with the other foot

Roll the outside of the foot over the ball and play it with the inside to the inside of the other foot. Give it a couple of taps and repeat with the other foot

Fast footwork
on the ball

Place the foot on the ball, make a quick turn, take the ball over with the other foot and play it forward with the inside of this foot. Give it a couple of taps and repeat the exercise with the other foot

Practising fast footwork in pairs, one player at a time

Roll the ball back and forth under the foot, tap it a couple of times and roll it back and forth under the other foot

Roll the ball away with the outside of the foot and with the inside of the same foot play it to the inside of the other. Give it a couple of taps and repeat with the other foot

Fast footwork on the ball

Draw the ball back and play it with the inside of the foot to the inside of the other. Give it a couple of taps and do the same thing with the other foot. You practise on one spot

Foot on the ball. As you are making a quick turn, take the ball over with the other foot and play it forward with the outside of the foot. Give it a couple of taps and repeat with the other foot

Draw the ball back with the toe, then draw it back with the inside of the other foot and play it forward with the outside of the instep of that foot. Give it a couple of taps and repeat with the other foot

Practising fast footwork in threes, with one player always resting

Fast footwork
on the ball

What you see on these pages are merely some examples, because the emphasis is on speed of footwork in all the forms in which the basic techniques are practised.

4. Looking beyond the ball

Footballers with technical limitations can never make fast plays because, even where there is no opponent, all their attention is on the ball. This means that they cannot survey the field. For this reason there is no point in technically limited players engaging in group games or combination forms in which the ball can be touched only once or twice. No coach or trainer needs to tell a football personality what to do in unpredictable match situations. These players take in the situation even before they have got possession. They scarcely pay any attention to the ball, yet they have it under control. This section provides a basis for achieving this by having players carry out all the techniques in the previous sections but looking as much as possible beyond the ball. This is also required of the players throughout the rest of the plan.

As soon as the players have mastered all the ball techniques they must practise carrying them out while looking beyond the ball

5. Feinting while in possession

Place the foot next to the ball. The moment the heel is alongside it, hit the ball with the inside of the foot against the inside of the other foot

The different ways of catching an opponent on the wrong foot by feinting are too numerous to be fitted into one book. Feinting is also used to win possession of the ball and to put an opponent who has the ball off balance. Unfortunately, teams consist almost exclusively of players who seldom if ever feint. This has made football more predictable and, hence, less attractive. A player who wants to be able to get past his man must know the basic techniques, but he must also learn how to feint. This should not be any problem once you have mastered the basic movements, because many of them are used in feinting as well as in other components of the game. You will see for yourself that any opponent reacts to a feint. Shortly you will be required to put as many feints as possible into practice. In time you will automatically begin to use the types of feints that suit you best and it will no longer even be possible to tell whether they are natural or acquired.

Pretend to be about to kick the ball but at the last moment take it forward with the outside of the kicking foot

Pretend to be about to kick but at the last moment pivot the ball under your body to the inside of the other foot

Feinting
while in possession

Pretend to be about to kick but tap the ball behind the supporting leg and take it away

Practising feinting

Step over the ball then play it forward with the inside of the other foot

Pretend to be breaking into a run but come back to the starting position

Feinting
while in possession

Pretend to be passing the ball but carry it along with the inside of the foot and take it over with the outside of the other foot

Pretend to be about to kick but at the last moment trap the ball, shield it with your body and take it away with the other foot

Pairs with two balls practising feinting

Pretend to be about to kick the ball but take it away with the outside of the foot

Feinting
while in possession

Pretend to backheel the ball but accelerate in a forward direction

Draw the ball back, then carry it forward with the outside of the instep of the same foot

Pretend to be about to play the ball with the inside of the foot. The foot stops over the top of the ball and you turn it behind the supporting leg

Practising feinting kicks

Feinting
while in possession

You pretend to pivot the ball inwards but put your foot behind it and flick it over the opponent's leg

Pretend to be about to kick the ball with the inside of the foot, but roll the foot over the ball and draw it back

Practising feinting with an opponent

Pretend to be about to kick but turn the ball under the body with the toe and carry it away in the opposite direction

All the feints can be executed in the practice forms used for the basic techniques. As soon as players have mastered them individually they are practised against an opponent

Practising feinting a kick

Feinting
while in possession

Players practising feints. Fixed pairs of players, each with a ball, practise the movements opposite one another in a free space. Then opponents take up positions and the players in possession practise against them at random

Feinting
while in possession

On this page: Players practising feints in the presence of an opponent

Opposite: Four players with two balls. The two players in possession make a feint and move sideways. The defenders keep on turning to face their new opponent

6. Creating and improvising

Roll the ball with the inside of the foot against the inside of the other foot, then draw the ball back and again roll it

Draw the ball back and play it forward with the outside of the foot, then step over it and play it forward again

Trap the ball, place the foot in front of it; you pretend that you are going to play the ball forward with the outside of the foot but play it with the outside of the other foot

These are merely three examples. The number of possibilities is infinite. All the ball techniques can be put to use

When you have learned to execute all the techniques perfectly at speed it is no longer necessary to practise them individually. The most important quality needed by a footballer is the ability to create and improvise. In no other sport does a player with the ball have so much scope to give free rein to his creative capacities. In training a footballer, therefore, creative and improvisational ability must be worked on right from the start. The game is crying out for players with fully developed creative capabilities. In this section, all the techniques must be practised in any combinations the player wishes.

Whether juniors or seniors, the players can indulge themselves to the full. In doing so they will discover ever more possibilities and moves with the ball, and the stimulus this provides will make them work at it all the harder. You must make sure, however, that the moves are not carried out in a monotonous tempo. Players must work with changes of rhythm.

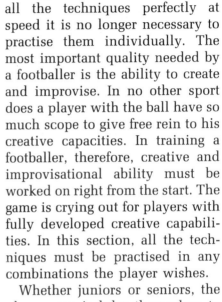

Practising creative and improvisational ability is the best individual training and it can also be done outside the official sessions as homework. Naturally, a player must also be able to create and improvise against opposition, which is why defenders are brought in

Creating
and improvising

The two players with the balls must try to lift them over the defender into the goal. At a later stage the defender can try to head the balls away from the goal

Working in pairs, the players put outswingers into the other goal

7. Kicking and trapping

The pairs of players with the balls must try to lift them diagonally over the defender into the other goal

The pair with the balls centre outswingers; the other two put them in past the near post. When all the balls have been used, the pairs switch jobs

Kicking technique cannot be practised effectively until the players have gone through the exercises in the previous sections. Kicking and trapping are above all a question of feel for the ball. This explains why all technically gifted players have a good kicking technique even though they have undergone no special training for it. Having a feel for the ball also makes it a lot easier to develop the player's weak leg, something which must be done, because in modern football players have neither the time nor the space to transfer the ball to their strong leg.

Kicking practice can take a varied form, with the trainer determining distance and intensity. In practising kicking techniques you automatically practise trapping. As kicking technique also forms part of the sections on receiving and coming away with the ball, getting past an opponent, making one-two combinations, shooting and heading, every player will acquire a good kicking technique without any trouble.

Six players form a circle. The two players in possession dribble the ball to the middle and play it on the turn to the next player

Left: The players at the back place deep diagonal balls. The players in the middle go for them, control them and make deep diagonal passes back

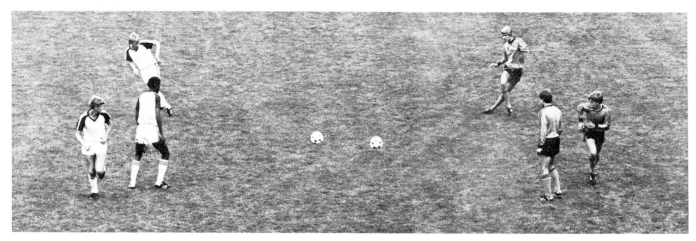

Kicking
and trapping

The player at the back lifts the ball over the head of the player in the middle; the front man plays it with one touch to the middle man, who takes it and changes places with the front man. He then lifts the ball over the middle man to the player at the back

Six players form a circle. They are divided into two groups of three with two balls, which they pass to one another. As a player passes one ball, the other is on its way to him. The same exercise can, of course, also be carried out with one group of three and two balls

The player at the back lifts the ball over the head of the middle player, gets it back immediately and moves to the front, where he receives the ball from the man who is now at the back. Then the same thing with four players and four balls, down the length of the field

The outside men play the balls to the inside men, who take them and play them back. The inside players then turn to receive the next ball from the other outside player

Kicking
and trapping

Two men with two balls kick them to each other simultaneously

Two pairs, overlapping, each player with a ball. The two members of each pair kick the balls simultaneously over the head of the member of the other pair who is standing between them

Three men, two balls. The man at the front plays the ball to the middle man, who receives it and takes up position next to the front man. The front man, meanwhile, receives the ball from the player at the back

Two groups of three, each group with one ball. The players with the ball pass it to another player in their group, who takes their place, where-upon they move sideways into the other group

Three players form a large triangle. A fourth player has the ball, which he kicks past one of the players on the inside while he sprints round him on the outside. He then passes the ball to that player and takes his place in the triangle. The player who now has the ball does the same thing with the next player in the triangle

Kicking
and trapping

Six players in a circle, two balls. The player with the ball passes it to the next but one in the circle, who passes it back to the player who has been missed. The latter again passes it to the next but one in the circle, and so on

The players with the balls kick them to their partners, who try to trap them in any way they can. When all the balls have been used up the partners switch jobs

Bryan Robson
A man of nerve

Bryan Robson is an outstanding example of the technical player who is also fearless. Robson cannot be cowed, neither by an opponent nor by the risk of injury.

As Alan Ball, of England's 1966 World Cup winners, put it: 'Bryan leads from the front. If there was a war, he would be the first charging out of the trenches.'

Robson fought back from two broken legs and a broken ankle inside a year at West Bromwich. At Manchester United, he has overcome serious damage to his shoulder, ankle, ligaments and tendons.

The long lay-offs haven't blurred his technique. He is rated among the best England captains as an almost unique combination of the old-time inside forward and wing-half.

He scores goals with his head and feet, he passes creatively, he tackles back – and his sudden long runs into the penalty area always scare defenders who last saw him in a harmless, deep position.

Robson's skills are enhanced by his courage. Young players should watch him and ask themselves: 'Could I do as he did once – play with fifteen fresh stitches in my arm?'

Phase 2 Dominating the opponent

1. *Receiving the ball and coming away with it*
2. *Shielding the ball*
3. *Dribbling the ball free*
4. *Group games*

The situation is determined now by the player with the ball, whose job it is to outplay his opponent

Now that you have discovered in the first phase that you can be successful with the ball you will have more of the inner stimulation required for your further development as a footballer. No doubt you have gained so much self-confidence that you are dying to use all the techniques you have learned to dominate an opponent. This is where the emphasis lies in the second phase. Ball possession must now be put to the best possible use; it must be retained by baffling your opponents. In this phase independence, flair and self-confidence are required. Colourless football is no longer acceptable; all of the techniques must be used to outplay your opponent. And the amount of resistance offered by that opponent will gradually be increased.

In the course of the exercises and games a player must practise all the ball techniques in order to discover which of them are best suited to a given situation in his case and with which of them he achieves most success.

Two players kick the balls diagonally and change places with the players who have received them

The outside players pass the balls to the inside players, who take them on the turn and pass them to the other outside player

1. Receiving the ball and coming away with it

In this section you learn to receive the ball and come away with it against opposition. You must use your body in a correct way and at the right moment feint or shoulder your opponent. The defenders must co-operate in giving everybody the opportunity to become skilled in this component of the game. The opposition offered by the defenders is gradually increased to one hundred per cent. The reasons for devoting special attention to this component lie in the close, hard marking in present-day football, the lack of space, the speed of the ball and the fact that it is often not possible to pass the ball immediately.

Three players with two balls form a square in which one corner is unoccupied. The player without a ball receives a pass and takes the ball to the unoccupied corner. The player who is now without a ball receives a pass. When they receive the ball the players can feint

The two in the middle compete for the ball. The winners pass the ball back and change places with each other and the balls are again played to the pairs in the middle

The men who put the balls into play change places with the winners of the duels, joining the losers in the middle

Receiving the ball
and coming away with it

The *winner of the duel comes away with the ball, then backheels it to the loser and joins the third player. The loser then plays the ball to them and a duel is fought between this new pair*

The *winner of the duel takes the ball to the place where it was put into play, thus forming a new pair. The loser plays the ball to the other pair*

The winners of the duels play the balls diagonally to the losers, then join the solo players to form new pairs. The losers then play the balls to the new pairs

Receiving the ball and coming away with it

The pairs in the middle compete for the balls. The winners take the balls in a backward direction, pass them to the outside players and take their places

The winner moves back with the ball. The man who has played it to the pair joins the loser and the winner then plays to the ball to them

The player interposes his body between the ball and his opponent at the right moment, making use of the basic techniques

The players in possession shield the ball, using whichever basic movement they choose

2. Shielding the ball

Good players always place their body between the ball and the opponent at the right moment, not only to shield the ball but also to permit a quick resumption of play. As all the basic techniques can be used in doing this, it can be practised in a highly varied way.

You can use both legs, which is a great advantage, while looking beyond the ball; suppleness and agility are also important. The exercises are enjoyable to do, with the player daring his opponent to come for the ball and then interposing his body at the right moment.

Naturally, when you come to apply what you have learned in match situations you will automatically use the techniques that suit you best.

Shielding the ball in a free space

Left: The defenders and the players in possession move freely among the group, with the players in possession continually placing their body between the ball and a defender at the right moment

Right: Pairs with one ball. The player in possession repeatedly goes to the defender and shields the ball by means of a basic movement

Pairs arranged in a circle. The players in possession work back and forth between two defenders

Shielding the ball

The players in possession take turns in approaching the defender. As soon as he goes for the ball they shield it and take up position again

Left: Pairs practising shielding the ball in turns

Groups of four with two balls. The outside players act as defenders. The players in possession work back and forth, constantly keeping their body between the ball and the defenders

Three players arrange themselves in a square with one unoccupied corner. The two players in possession take turns in moving to the unoccupied corner, but there they encounter the defender. They shield the ball and go back to their own corner

Shielding the ball against full opposition

Shielding the
ball

Three pairs, each with one ball, arrange themselves in a triangle. The players in possession work around the triangle, shielding the ball with a basic movement when they come to a defender

Two pairs, each with one ball. The players in possession work back and forth, the other two players acting as defenders

Same set-up, but now you make for the unoccupied corner after the ball has been passed to you

The player in possession darts explosively past the defender

Three players with two balls in a square with one unoccupied corner. The players in possession set off in turns for the unoccupied corner, where they encounter a defender. They beat the defender by means of a basic technique and take his place

3. Dribbling the ball free

The ability to shake off opponents by dribbling is one of the most important attributes needed by a player if he is to play attractive football. It is difficult to reach players with long passes and as soon as you try to run with the ball you encounter an opponent. In situations like this most players avoid taking any risks by passing the ball on to a team-mate or kicking it upfield at random, which usually results in loss of possession.

If dull uniformity is to be avoided in footballers it is essential that this aspect of the game should be practised with courage and without the fear of failure. What has been learned about shielding the ball can be put to good use here, as can all the basic techniques and feints. As soon as you have beaten your direct opponent you move upfield with the ball at your feet. The best possible use must be made of ball possession every time. In this section the players must continually dribble the ball free, shield it, move up with it and apply the basic and feinting techniques. If these things are not repeated endlessly in practice they will never be used in a game.

After the player in possession has beaten his opponent he passes the ball to the neutral player, who has meanwhile passed his ball to the defender. He in turn tries to beat the defender who is coming for him

The player in possession tries to dribble the ball over the line, while the defender tries to stop him

Two attackers take turns in trying to dribble the ball over the line, which is guarded by a single defender

Three attackers and three defenders engage in one-against-one duels in turns

As soon as an attacker loses the ball he becomes a defender

Dribbling
the ball free

Two groups of three, facing one another. The players in possession use a basic technique to beat the defenders as they come in. They then return the ball and become defenders

Two groups of three. The players in possession force back the defenders, who offer graduated amounts of resistance. The players switch roles, and so on

Two pairs play one against one in a demarcated area. The players can score by dribbling the ball over the imaginary line. After a while the players in the middle change places with the other four

Two pairs play one against one in a demarcated area. As soon as a player loses the ball he drops out to rest. The waiting player comes in fresh as the defender and the defender takes on the role of attacker

Dribbling
the ball free

One against one in a demarcated area. The winners always play against one another

Three pairs play one against one in a demarcated area. Players can score by dribbling the ball over the imaginary line

Three pairs play one against one in a demarcated area

Two against two with one neutral player, in a demarcated area. Players can score by dribbling the ball over the imaginary line

Two against two in a demarcated area. Players can score by dribbling the ball over the imaginary line. The player who scores retains possession

One against one in a demarcated area with two neutral one-touch line assistants. The players in the middle must make as many individual moves as possible and can score by dribbling the ball over the imaginary line. The player in possession may make use of the services of the assistants for passing purposes, while the assistants may also pass to each other. After a given number of plays, the two in the middle change places with the two assistants

4. Group games

Three against three. The player in possession uses basic and feinting techniques. Players can score by dribbling the ball over the imaginary line

Right: Two against two with two neutral assistants in a demarcated area. Players in possession must make as many individual moves as possible. The assistants are allowed to pass to one another. Continuous switching of roles

Now that the players have developed skill with the ball, as well with as without an opponent, they can start playing games. The numbers in the games must be kept small in order to ensure that players are in possession as often as possible. The emphasis in the games is on individual moves. Players who play monotonously and simply pass the ball on to team-mates without trying anything themselves are punished by being made to run round the pitch. This is repeated until such time as they come to realize that they will never become good footballers by passing the ball on whenever they get it. All energy and positive aggressiveness must be put into individual play.

Only when you are capable of undertaking something on your own can you develop into a football personality. It does not matter if individual moves lead to loss of possession in the beginning. This is still where the emphasis must be placed.

The players now possess sufficient technical and creative qualities that to have possession of the ball and not use it is a waste.

The defenders must save as much of their strength as possible by making their opposition as flexible as possible. In time the players will automatically discover which techniques they are most

Four against two. The player in possession has to touch the ball at least three times before passing. If he loses possession he switches with a defender

117

One against one with four neutral one-touch line assistants

Two pairs play one against one with four neutral assistants. Players can score by dribbling the ball over the imaginary line

Two against two with one neutral player. Players can score by passing the ball to their partner between two cones

Group games

Two against two with four neutral assistants. Alternating roles

successful with, while their capacity for observing and reacting and their timing will be developed without effort.

Such games can also be played outside the club sessions, and trainers should encourage this. Meanwhile, trainers who prohibit individual play should keep their hands off young players.

Three against three with the emphasis on individual play when in possession. Players can score by passing the ball to one of their team-mates between the two cones

One against one with one neutral player and two neutral assistants. The neutral player and the assistants are only allowed to touch the ball once. The two players must engage in as much individual play as possible. They can score by dribbling the ball over the imaginary line

Frans Thijssen
Confidence brings success

Frans Thijssen was voted England's Footballer of the Year in 1981. He was the first foreign winner since Bert Trautmann, Manchester City's acrobatic German goalkeeper, in 1956.

Yet Ipswich Town didn't appreciate at first that Thijssen was the world's best at high-speed, mazy dribbling, as well as a specialist in the disconcerting dead-stop.

He recalled: 'I struggled early on at Ipswich because they kept playing the ball over my head to the front two.'

Thijssen also overcame hard times in Holland before winning a place in the national team. He had to work for success after joining NEC Nijmegen, his home-town club, as only an average seventeen-year old.

He was a quiet youngster, almost tongue-tied – but he was also level-headed, ambitious and willing to put in hours of unsupervised practice. So he mastered the techniques and that achievement gave him confidence.

Self-confidence brought success.

Phase 3

Beating and bypassing opponents

1. *Techniques for beating an opponent*
2. *Practising the techniques with opposition*
3. *Beating an opponent with a one-two combination*
4. *Through passes*
5. *Group games*

In the first phase you devoted all your energy to becoming as skilful and many-sided as possible in possession. In the second phase these techniques were used to outplay an opponent. By now you have a reasonable technical basis, and because certain techniques are working better and better, inner stimulation and inspiration will play an increasingly important part in your further development. You feel that you are becoming more self-

confident with the ball and now you want to do more. In this phase you must have the self-confidence and flair needed to beat your man or bypass him by means of a one-two combination.

The fact that you now have mastery over your body and the ball means that you can also master your opponent. In this phase you have the opportunity to get past an opponent by dribbling or using a one-two combination. Make use of it. This does not apply only to attackers, because the ability to get past an opponent is also extremely important in a midfielder or a defender. Without this ability you will always be a limited player, unable to create chances or manoeuvre team-mates into the kind of positions that produce goals. Only top players force openings through individual play. Without such individual capacities they would be helpless, no different from all the average players. Most players are not even capable of getting past an opponent even with someone to help them. When they are faced with a superior defensive force in the penalty area they are completely impotent. Even highly expensive attackers are neutralized without any trouble by a personal marker if they don't receive any help in the form of team-mates able to run onto a pass placed behind the defenders.

All too often you see a defender pass the ball to a forward with a marker behind him. That is one possibility, but the situation becomes much more interesting if the

defender can beat his opponent and then combine his creative abilities with those of the forward to shake off the latter's marker. Simply getting rid of the ball to a team-mate has never yet produced an interesting situation in a game of football.

1. Techniques for beating an opponent

With spring in your supporting leg, draw the ball towards you with the inside of the other foot, then take it away explosively with the outside of that foot

The same exercise except that you use the outside of the foot to flick the ball over the imaginary leg of an opponent

Again the same exercise, but instead of playing the ball with the outside of the same foot you step sideways and take the ball away with the outside of the other foot

You scarcely ever see a player beat an opponent on his own nowadays, even though it is precisely things like this that the public come to see. Even worse, you never see players practising the techniques for beating an opponent, which means that trainer-coaches either do not have command of the techniques or don't consider them to be important. Personally, I'm more inclined to believe the former. I see these coaches become indignant when a player loses the ball trying to get past an opponent, but nothing at all is said about players who simply get rid of the ball to a team-mate, which is what is emptying the stands, or about players who lose the ball through bad passing. Many coaches even go so far as to forbid gifted players to beat their man on their own. If the great football personalities of the past had been treated in the same way they would never have emerged from the ranks of the nondescript.

Any normally gifted footballer can learn every technique for beating a man. And they can be learned all the easier after the improvement in co-ordination achieved in the preceding phases. Another advantage is that the basic techniques and feints can now be used for getting past an opponent. Like the others, the techniques for beating a man should be practised as often as possible, until they have been perfectly mastered. The amount of resistance offered by the opponent is then increased

Techniques
for beating an opponent

The scissors. Step over the ball with your left foot and take the ball away explosively with the outside of the other foot

gradually. Finally, all of the techniques are used in a variety of group games against full opposition. This will enable you to discover for yourself which techniques are best suited to you. Once you achieve success with particular techniques you continue to use them. When you have finally mastered the art of beating your opponent at the right moment you will be worth more to your team than ten ball-passers together.

The same exercise except that now you step over the ball with your right foot and take it away with the outside of your left

Double scissors. Step over the ball quickly with your left foot, then with your right, and take it away explosively with the outside of your left foot

The player in possession beats his opponent, then passes to the third player, who in turn beats him and passes to the other player

Techniques
for beating an opponent

The scissors round the ball. Step round the ball and take the ball away with the outside of your other foot

The player in possession beats his opponent, then stops the ball and switches to the role of defender

Pretend to be going past your opponent to the right, then take the ball away explosively with the outside of your left foot

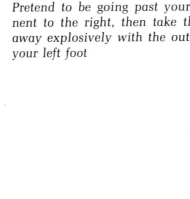

Step sideways over the ball with your left foot, then take it away with the outside of your right foot

Techniques
for beating an opponent

You pretend to be about to pivot the ball inwards but take it away explosively with the outside of the same foot

Players taking turns to practise the techniques in the presence of an opponent

Pretend to be about to pivot the ball with your left foot, but take it away with your right

You pretend to be going to the right by tapping the ball with the inside of your left foot to the inside of your right, then set off in the opposite direction

Techniques
for beating an opponent

Pretend to be about to play the ball past your opponent with your right foot, then draw the ball across your body and take it past him with the inside of the other foot

Pretend to be about to pivot the ball with your right foot, but move your foot to the side of the ball and take it away with the outside of your left foot

The defenders try to dispossess the attackers

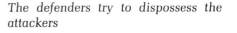

Take a long step over the ball with your left leg, thus shielding it from your opponent, then turn it away from him using the outside of your right foot

Practising the techniques for beating an opponent in a zigzag pattern, back and forth

Two groups of players, each player with a ball. Two players practise the techniques, then go to the back of the line

2. Practising the techniques with opposition

The scissors, with the player playing the ball past his opponent with the outside of his other foot

With spring in your supporting leg, draw the ball towards you with the inside of the foot, then play it quickly past your opponent with the outside of the foot

All the techniques must be practised with an opponent. The player in possession steps over the ball and then takes it away with the instep of his other foot, which places his body between the ball and his opponent

Threes with one ball. The player in possession beats his opponent and passes the ball to the third player, whom he then challenges in the role of defender

The middle player receives the ball, turns with it and beats the third player. He then passes it to the third player, who turns with it and beats the first

Threes with two balls. Two players practise the techniques for beating an opponent. The one facing the third player then passes his ball to him, whereupon the third player joins the other player with a ball, who has turned to face him

Practising the techniques with opposition

The players beat their opponents, then play the ball back and become defenders

Each of the players has a ball and they take turns in beating one another

Four players with two balls arrange themselves in a triangle. The player in possession beats an opponent, who then receives the other ball and beats the next player

The same set-up, but now the players tap the ball past their opponent on one side and run round him on the other

Four players form a square. Two of them receive balls from two defenders, whom they then beat. Having done this they pass the balls to the next players and become defenders

Threes with two balls. The player in possession who is nearest the man without a ball beats him. The defender then receives the other ball and becomes the attacker

Practising the techniques with opposition

Threes with two balls. The players in possession take turns in beating the defender. A player who fails to beat him becomes the defender

Four players in possession beat two defenders, one after the other. Players who fail become defenders

Four players in possession beat two defenders in turn. Players who fail become defenders

Three players, one of whom receives a ball from a fourth player, beats his opponent and passes the ball back to the fourth player. The defender has meanwhile received a ball from the fourth player and beats the man facing him

When he has been beaten, the defender receives a ball from the man at the back and beats the player in front of him

Two players in possession try to beat two defenders and dribble the ball over the line. The other two players with balls then pass them to the defenders, who try to dribble them over the other line

Practising the techniques with opposition

Three players with two balls take it in turns to beat an opponent standing in the middle. The ball is then lobbed back to the waiting player

Two players in possession and one defender. The two in possession take it in turns to beat the defender by flicking the ball over his right leg, then left leg

Three players in possession take turns in trying to beat a defender. A player who fails becomes the defender

The player in possession beats the defender by dribbling or with a one-two combination. After a given number of plays the three switch roles

Two defenders, two one-touch assistants and three players who take turns in beating the defenders by dribbling or with a one-two combination. A player who loses possession becomes a defender

3. Beating an opponent with a one-two combination

The player in possession gets past his opponent with a one-two combination. He then passes the ball to his partner in the combination, who beats him by dribbling or making a one-two combination with the third player

The player in possession tries to beat his opponent as often as possible by dribbling or making a one-two combination. When he loses possession the players switch roles

Beating an opponent becomes really easy when a team-mate presents himself at the right moment for a one-two combination. After dribbling, the best way of getting past one or more opponents is a one-two combination. Unfortunately, successful one-two combinations are also becoming an increasingly rare sight. The reasons for this lie in tough man-to-man marking, the speed of play and lack of space, but also in the players' limited technical abilities.

Trainers must come to realize that all their practising against posts and passive opponents is completely pointless. A successful one-two combination requires two players with football intelligence and a feel for the ball, neither of which you can acquire by practising one-two combinations against a

The three players in white shirts take turns in beating the second defender by dribbling or making a one-two combination. They then beat the first defender, with the second defender assisting in the one-two combinations

Three players with two balls take turns in beating their opponent by dribbling or making one-two combinations with one of the two one-touch assistants in white shirts. When the defender is beaten he receives the other ball and becomes the attacker

Left: The ball is passed to the marked player, who returns it with one touch. The first player then either beats the marker by dribbling or plays a deep pass to his sprinting partner

Beating an opponent with a one-two combination

The player in the foregound lobs the ball to his partner and positions himself for a one-two combination. The player in the background then lobs the ball and positions himself for a one-two combination. A player who loses the ball becomes the defender

Below: Three players, each with a ball, take turns in beating the defender by dribbling or making a one-two combination. A player who loses the ball becomes the defender

post. The second player must have various options, and in many cases he will have to pass to someone else. This is practised particularly in the group games at the end of this section.

Once you have mastered the techniques for beating a man and have also acquired the football intelligence and feel for the ball required for a perfect one-two combination you will have no need to fear any defender. In the different

The player in possession beats his opponent and passes to the third player. The neutral assistant is available for one-two combinations

Player makes a one-two combination with the furthest player, who then receives a lob from the other side and makes either a long or a short one-two combination

Five players, two of them in the middle. The first player in the middle receives the ball and hits it back first time. The second player is beaten either by dribbling or by a one-two combination

Beating an opponent
with a one-two combination

Repeated one-two combinations, with the players in the middle alternately acting as defender and assistant for the combinations

The player in dark shorts gets past his opponent either by beating him or with a one-two combination and takes up position beyond the defender. The other defender then plays the ball to the other player in dark shorts, who in turn gets past his opponent either by beating him or with a one-two combination and takes up position beyond him

group games and competitive forms of practice the defenders must do everything possible to intercept the ball. If they succeed, they are rewarded with possession and it is then their turn to try to get past the defenders. In practising one-two combinations the value of being able to look beyond the ball will become evident.

Two players get past the defender by means of a one-two combination. The defender then receives the ball from the player in the foreground and beats him. The defender receives the ball from the other end and chooses between beating his man and a one-two combination

Three players take turns in getting past a defender by beating him or making use of a long one-two combination. A player who loses the ball becomes the defender

Two defenders try to prevent the attackers, in white shirts, crossing the imaginary line by beating their man or making a one-two combination with the player behind the line. The players in the dark shorts then pass their balls to the defenders, who become the attackers and try to do the same thing

The player in the foreground lofts the ball over the defender. He takes up position and the player with the ball gets past the defender either by beating him or by making use of a one-two combination. The first player then takes up position next to the defender, who receives the ball from the player at the back

Beating an opponent
with a one-two combination

The player at the back must get past the two defenders, in the light shirts, by dribbling or by means of a short or long one-two combination

Three players take turns in trying to get past two defenders, either by dribbling or by means of a short or long one-two combination

The player in possession beats his opponent or passes to the player coming up in support. The defender then receives the other ball and the player behind him without a ball acts as the supporting player

Left: Three pairs, each with a ball. The player without a ball takes up position as a defender; once he has performed his task as a defender, his partner, who is behind him with a ball, sets off and he becomes the supporting player

Pairs take turns in trying to get past a defender by beating him or playing a through pass to the player coming up in support

4. Timing through passes

Players running between or round defenders to take a through pass are almost unstoppable provided the timing is right. The defenders have their backs to the goal and are concentrating on the player with the ball. This means that players who are coming through at speed to take a good pass are extremely difficult to deal with despite the presence of a sweeper. There is always panic of some kind in the defence, and the positional changes that take place create new openings. It is an ideal weapon, yet one that is far too seldom used, because trainers do not pay enough attention to it.

As with almost all the other components, you can practise this in a variety of group games and competitive forms of training until strikers and midfielders can be certain that supporting players will be sprinting past them as soon as they get possession of the ball.

A player who makes too little use of this dangerous weapon must be made the neutral player, which means that he will be continually sprinting past the man in possession to defeat one defender after another.

Three pairs take turns in trying to get past each other using dribbling and passes to the supporting player

Two against two, the aim being to dribble the ball over the line. The neutral player acts as a supporting player, coming up to take through passes from whichever side is in possession

Two pairs. With the help of a neutral player, the pair in possession try to get past their opponents as often as possible by dribbling and passing to players coming up in support

One against one, with two neutral one-touch line assistants. The players must beat their man and make one-two combinations as often as possible. The game can also be played with the object of dribbling the ball over the line. Players and assistants repeatedly switch roles

Two against two with one neutral player. A team gets one point every time they get past their opponents by dribbling or a successful one-two combination. The game is then played with the object of dribbling the ball over the line, with the scoring team remaining in possession

One against one with four neutral one-touch line assistants. If the players in the middle cannot receive a pass the assistants can pass to one another

5. Group games

Two against two, with two one-touch line assistants, with as much dribbling and as many one-two combinations as possible

At the end of the second phase, every time they were in possession players had to apply techniques they had learned to get past their opponents. Every opportunity provided by possession must be used to beat one or more opponents. In doing so players automatically improve their mastery of techniques that have been acquired so far.

Lack of independence and personality are not accepted. You have to realize that you must become somebody as a footballer, otherwise you will not achieve the

Two pairs play one against one, with four assistants. The players in the middle must exercise their creative capacities to the full

Four against two. The four must make as many one-two combinations as possible

principal objective of this training plan. When you are in possession of the ball unchallenged, rather than simply get rid of it to a team-mate you must take the ball to an opponent and try to beat him in whatever way you choose. You can indulge your creative powers even more than in the earlier games, and in doing this you will improve your grasp of the game, your powers of observation and your ability to react. Particularly suitable here are games with one or more assistants, because they make the games

151

Two against two, with four one-touch line assistants

Left: Three pairs, with two assistants. The first pair try to dribble the ball over the line. The ball is then played to the defenders, who try to dribble the ball over the line defended by the third pair

Two against two, with four assistants who can operate over the entire line between the cones. If there is no player in a position to receive a pass the assistants can pass to each other

Group games

Three against three, with three one-touch assistants, the assistants repeatedly swopping places with one of the teams. The object is for players to exercise their creative powers to the full

Left: Three against three, with two assistants. The aim is to dribble the ball as often as possible over the opponents' line. A team which does so retains possession of the ball

more stimulating for the players and permit substitutions to be made when players tire. When you play a game with one, two, three or four assistants you gradually begin to feel that you are becoming somebody as a footballer. The days when you were merely a ball-passer have gone for ever. You now have command of all the techniques needed to get past defenders: by making full use of them you improve your grasp of the game, with the result that you become increasingly important to your team.

Three groups of three. Two teams play against each other. Two members of the third group act as assistants; the third is a neutral player and supports the team in possession. The aim is for the teams to dribble the ball over the line as often as possible, using their creative powers to the full. A team which scores retains possession

Gary Stevens
The versatile footballer

The versatile footballer is always sure of finding a club – and, because changes are always being forced by injuries, suspensions and loss of form, the versatile player can usually get a game.

Tom Finney, of Preston North End and England, was a byword for versatility in early post-war football for he could play marvellously on either wing and at centre forward.

John Charles, of Leeds, Juventus and Wales, was a sensation at centre-half and centre-forward in the sixties, but the modern all-rounder isn't expected to fill such contrasting roles. Instead, today's utility player might play in attack or in midfield – like Gary Stevens, of Tottenham Hotspur, in defence and midfield.

Stevens has played centre-half in a Wembley final for Brighton. He has played right-back for Tottenham, also sweeper and as the right-sided midfielder. England have also used him on the left of midfield.

Young all-rounders should study Stevens, noting particularly the comfortable touch on the ball that has brought him to prominence.

Phase 4

Creating chances and making use of them

1. *Shooting*
2. *Heading*
3. *Individual play*
4. *Group games*

Only now do we come to the finishing touches. The reason is that only when you have mastered all the techniques can you create chances without resorting to kick-and-rush football. Players train daily in the goal area, yet in matches you seldom see chances created by means of attacking techniques. Most players do not have them at their command, despite which they have to deal with a wall of defenders in top condition. It is necessary to go through the

previous sections first in order to acquire the mastery of attacking techniques needed to create chances.

A player who has done so will not only have the will to get to the goal; he will also be capable of getting past defenders by dribbling and passing, and he will want to score. The hesitant ball-passer will have made way for the self-confident, technically gifted and assertive attacker.

Where things have to happen is above all in the opponents' penalty area. This is where matches are decided and it is what happens here that draws the crowds.

Every young footballer should have played attacking football in the course of his training so that he will know what it is. Later, in matches, he must pose a threat when he is in possession of the ball. This is the only thing that can save football.

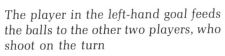

Shooting. Pay attention to technique and hit the ball cleanly

The player in the left-hand goal feeds the balls to the other two players, who shoot on the turn

1. Shooting

In modern football chances have to be used. As fewer and fewer chances are being created, players must be able to shoot with both feet from any angle and any position, because goals mean success and success draws the crowds.

What a player does with the chances he gets is decisive. A goal gives a player wings, whereas a missed opportunity can depress the whole team.

Normally speaking, every footballer ought to be able to shoot well, because scoring goals is the most important thing in the game. In practice, unfortunately, this is not the case; few players can shoot well with both feet and most players need time and space even to shoot with their strong foot.

Shots from the second line are a thing of the past. Professionals, who are able to train all day, are not even capable of a good shot at goal from the second line. This is incomprehensible, because the technique can be learned fairly rapidly merely with two goals and some balls. From this moment on, players must practise shooting every day.

The player in goal feeds the other two, who flick the ball up and shoot on the turn into the other goal

The keepers feed the players, who take the passes and shoot at goal. After each shot they receive the ball from the other keeper

The man in goal plays the balls alternately to the right and left of the man in the middle, who shoots alternately with his right and left foot

Left: The man in goal plays the ball to the man in the dark shorts; he taps it on to the third player, who shoots. The two in the middle switch roles every time

The man in goal feeds the other two players, who shoot in turn. The goals can be continually shifted, enabling trainers to keep on varying the type of practice

Shooting

Above: The player behind the goal throws the balls over it and the other shoots

Left: The man behind the goal plays the balls to the man next to it, who centres first time, and the third player shoots

The man in goal feeds the balls sideways and the other two players shoot in turn

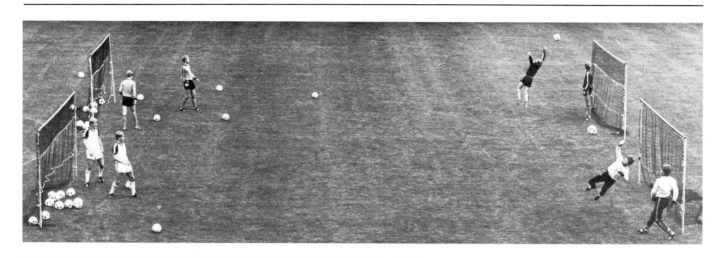

Two players take turns to shoot at two keepers, who take turns in goal

Left: The players behind the goals centre and the other two players shoot. Roles are changed when all the balls have been worked through

Two players take turns in centring, while the other two shoot inside the near post

Shooting

The two players at the sides feed the balls. The three players near the furthest goal shoot

The players in the goals feed the balls diagonally along the ground or through the air. The other players shoot on the turn

The players in the side goals feed the balls. The players in the middle shoot on the turn into the centre goals

Left: The players in the side goals feed the balls sideways to the other players, who shoot from long range

The balls are in the goals in the centre. From there the players do a short dribble and shoot

Shooting

The players in the goals with the balls feed them to players running up towards the goal, who shoot, then run behind the goal and then again towards it for their next shot

The men in the two nearest goals take turns in feeding balls to players coming up, who shoot into the two furthest goals

The balls are thrown from behind the goals. The four players take turns at heading in and constantly change goal

Heading from a stationary position, jumping with both legs

The keepers throw the balls to the players in a variety of different ways. Three players take turns at heading in, moving on to the other group after they have had their turn

2. Heading

Players behind the goal throw the balls, which two players head in turn

The players behind the goals throw the balls diagonally to the other players, who head in

If the opposing team are playing defensively the only room left is in the air, which is why heading is becoming increasingly important. More and more goals are the direct or indirect result of duels in the air. English football proves that heading duels in the goalmouth are unquestionably spectacular. High balls across the goal are much more attractive to spectators than the endless interpassing that goes on in midfield. Throughout the world huge sums of money are paid for heading specialists, the reason being that there are very few players who are good in the air when they are marked by an opponent. These match situations require a realistic form of training, with the players learning to jump with either leg or with both together.

Realistic heading training is particularly important for young players because it also develops their jumping power. For this reason the mobile goals shown here are very handy in that they can also be used for all sorts of heading games. These goals must be present at all times on any training field in order to allow players to work individually before and after sessions.

The keepers throw the balls. The players come in alternately from the right and the left, jumping with their left leg and right leg respectively

The player at the back lobs the ball over the middle player to the player in the foreground, who heads the ball to the feet of the first player as he runs forward. This player then takes up position at the front

The player in the foreground lobs the ball for the player at the back, who heads it to the feet of the first player as he runs past the middle player. He then takes up position at the back

Heading

Two players centre, the other two head the balls in

One player (not visible in the photograph) centres and two players go up for the ball, each trying to score. The other two players duel for the next ball

The players with the balls centre them and the other players head them in

One against one with two neutral players (white shirts). A player who scores retains possession

In the foreground, two against two with one neutral player. In the background, three against three, one of the players of the team not in possession acting as goalkeeper

Four against four with four goals. No handling is allowed and goals can be scored only by heading

Heading

The players in the goals on the left centre the balls diagonally. The other players, in twos, compete with each other to head in

The men behind the goals throw the balls, which the pairs in the middle try to head in, starting one behind the other and alongside each other

The keepers throw the balls. Two players take turns in trying to beat the permanent defender in the air, coming in from the right and the left

The players each get a ball from the keeper (right), beat an opponent and score. They then become defenders and the defenders become attackers

Left: The keepers kick the balls over the defenders to the attackers, who make a solo run and score. The keepers at the other end then kick the balls to the defenders, who now become attackers

Two players in possession beat their opponents and score. The balls are then passed to the defenders, who attack the other goal

3. Individual play

Two attackers set out in turns from the goal and are opposed by a defender

Right: One against one with a neutral assistant to return passes. The player who scores becomes the assistant and the assistant becomes the defender

The individual moves from the second and third phases can be used in trying to score. The player receives a pass with a man marking him, and it is then one against one

A game's entertainment value for the spectators is determined by individual play. Players who are capable of individual initiatives create decisive openings, and when players of this kind cap a solo run with a goal the crowds are really thrilled. In the years which are of so much importance for their future, young players must become masters of individual play in order to ensure that they do not vanish into the ranks of the nondescript. There is no more gratifying job for a trainer, because there is nothing young players like better than dribbling and scoring. By making one individual play after another, without any conscious effort players acquire a better grasp of the game and come to realize that individual moves produce more results and more goal opportunities than simply passing the ball on to a team-mate.

There is no way that players without individual qualities can raise themselves above the rank and file. Outside the penalty area there is ample room for individual play; inside the penalty area fast footwork is essential. As players are being given less and less time and space to shoot and make combinations, the speed with which they act is decisive.

In this section too, all of the different forms of practice can be used, while the mobile goals can be set up in a variety of arrangements.

Three against three, the object being to score

Three against three, or four against four, with four goals

Three against three with three goals, one for one team and two for the other. If there are not enough keepers, one of the team goes in goal

4. Group games

The players have now mastered all of the techniques needed in this section to create chances and score. You must have command of all the techniques before playing games with big goals, otherwise they don't have much point. Proof of this is that footballers are as limited at the end of their career as they were at the beginning. Though they play year in year out they cannot develop, because they have not mastered the techniques needed. Now that you have command of the techniques and have

Top: The handy thing about goals with straight nets is that two games can be played with three of them

Left: Four against four with four goals. There are keepers in two of them. In the other two, goals can only be scored with the head

Three against three in a demarcated area. A player who crosses the imaginary line shoots as soon as possible

Three pairs take turns in trying to get past one another. One pair defends the imaginary line. Once this has been crossed the player must shoot as quickly as possible. The defenders then receive the ball from the other end and become attackers

Left: Four against four with four goals. There are three groups of four in total, with the groups taking turns to provide the keepers

The same, except that now it is three against three with one neutral player. The winner is the team that scores the most goals in succession

Group games

shot at goal from every angle and position, you can give free play to your creativity in a game.

In every type of game players must use all of the techniques they have learned and the amount of opposition must gradually be increased. Games with several goals are a particularly good way for players to exercise their powers. If a player in possession persists in playing unimaginatively the ball is forfeited to the opposing team, because colourless football is now definitely taboo.

Top: Three groups of three, one group resting while the other two play against each other. When a team scores they retain possession

Left: Three against three with a neutral assistant on the imaginary line

Four against four. Goals can be scored either by putting the ball into one of the two nets or by dribbling it over the imaginary line. The scoring team retain possession

Kenny Dalglish
Born to greatness

'Och, just put him on the park and let him play', said Jock Stein when asked about what might be Kenny Dalglish's best position.

Stein, who managed Celtic to nine Scottish championships, sold Dalglish to Liverpool as a replacement for Hamburg-bound Kevin Keegan in 1977.

The fee of £440,000 doubled the Liverpool record but was soon seen as a bargain for a born footballer who had been capped by Scotland after only sixteen League games and who was destined to become the first to score 100 League goals in both Scotland and England.

Former Liverpool manager Bob Paisley calls Dalglish: 'The best player in my forty-six years at Anfield. From the start, he read my team better than they understood him.'

Dalglish is sturdy with squat, sprinting thighs, a build which helps him to turn quickly while also making him uncommonly difficult to knock off the ball.

Young players should try to copy that turning technique while also striving to match three of Dalglish's other qualities:

unselfish awareness

dedication and

utter modesty.

Phase 5

Physical condition

1. *Agility and flexibility*
2. *Basic stamina*
3. *Speed*
4. *Stamina and speed of play*
5. *Explosive power*

In the fifth phase extra attention is paid to players' physical condition, but all the techniques which have been learned so far are gone through again. The trainer decides the intensity, the number of repetitions, the duration and the rest periods.

Almost everywhere condition training is of an unrealistic kind. Were this not so, for years now football would have been dominated by the eastern bloc countries. Running and sprinting in accordance with scientific training programmes do not make you a football personality, merely a superfit player with a minimum of creative technical ability

Though a football trainer ought to have some basic knowledge of physiology it certainly isn't necessary for him to be able to recite the Latin names of all the muscles. What he does need is a thorough knowledge of realistic exercises for increasing the co-ordination, speed, explosive power and stamina of footballers. Far too often one

sees players being driven about like a herd by a trainer's whistle and performing all sorts of exercises in which there is no trace of independence or personality.

It is perfectly all right to subject technically gifted players to the old-fashioned condition training once in a while, but for technically limited players to waste costly time with such soul-destroying routines is wrong. Condition training, like other forms of training, must be match-orientated. It must be such that players improve their technical skills and simultaneously develop an optimal condition for playing a game of football.

Agility and flexibility

The literature on training is overflowing with unrealistic forms of exercise to develop a footballer's agility and flexibility. What one sees in practice, however, is that after ten years of such exercises a player is still angular and uneconomical in his movements, which says all that needs to be said about the utility of the exercises in question.

Even a trained gymnast would look clumsy practising the ball techniques, because he does not have the necessary co-ordination. The only way you can acquire the co-ordination and suppleness needed is by constant training with the ball.

This will give you optimal flexibility in the ankle and hip joints and it will also develop flexibility of the spine (turning). The only joint for which there is an abun-

dance of exercises in the specialist literature is the shoulder joint, which is less important for footballers.

Basic stamina

In recent years sportsmen have been working on their basic stamina by running ever longer distances, with the emphasis more on duration than on speed and intensity. In this type of training the pulse rate varies between 130 and 140 beats a minute. Heart volume, respiration and blood flow are developed, and these are the things which largely determine stamina.

Heart volume is the amount of blood that the heart pumps through the body per minute. The more blood is pumped through the body per minute, the more oxygen is supplied to the muscles and, hence, the more work they can perform. The body also recovers more rapidly from effort.

Distance running is unnecessary, because basic stamina can be improved by practising the ball techniques. What the trainer must do is have the players practise the ball techniques in such a way that the heartbeat fluctuates between 130 and 140 per minute. They will then be improving their technical skills at the same time as achieving excellent results as regards stamina.

Speed

The only problem area in developing a player's physical qualities is sprinting speed. For the most part this is inherited. Even an ideal programme of sprint training will not give a slow player the speed of a natural sprinter. In football, however, speed does not only mean speed in a sprint. The main thing a footballer needs is the ability to make decisive moves in a game, and this is something that any player who follows this training plan can achieve, because it will greatly improve his tactical insight. Slow players, therefore, need not despair. There are masses of fast players who cannot make fast, decisive moves for want of the techniques and tactical skills needed in possession. You must become as dynamic a footballer as possible, someone who is capable, when circumstances allow, of rapidly setting constructive moves in motion. A lot of attention needs to be paid to speed, particularly in youngsters between the ages of thirteen and sixteen. All of the exercises can now be practised at speed and the emphasis can also be put on speed in group games.

There is no point in training for speed when you haven't yet recovered from your previous exertions. The various exercises and competitive forms of practice should therefore be carried out with three or four players to ensure that they have adequate rest.

Stamina and speed of play

All the exercises and competitive forms of practice can be used to raise the pulse rate to 170-180 beats a minute. Duration, intensity, number of repetitions and rest periods can be determined by the trainer, who can gradually increase the various components.

The enthusiasm among the players will be so great that, contrary to the situation with the usual condition training without a ball, they will need restraining rather than encouraging. It is very important that the trainer should be alert to the fact that young players in particular must have sufficient rest between exercises. The rest periods can be used for ball exercises requiring little effort. Trainers with a capacity for improvisation can put it to good use here.

Four players move around a square, playing the balls past the cones on the inside and sprinting around them on the outside. All kinds of movements can also be practised at the cones. The players are replaced two at a time by the two that are resting

Three players with one ball. The first player sprints a certain number of yards with the ball at his feet, stops it and plays it back. The second player does as the first. The third player runs half the distance, returns to where he started from and passes the ball across to the first player, who does as before

Physical condition

Players in possession pass the balls to the players on the other side and sprint after them. Repeat three times. Left: The players with the balls can either pass them back or leave them at the cones and sprint back to their places. Depending on what the first two have done, the second pair either take the balls to the cones or collect them there. Players can incorporate all kinds of movements into the exercise. Below: Two groups of three with two balls. Players with the balls sprint to the other side and pass them back. All sorts of variations are possible later. Players in possession can go through all the movements in the middle

Three players form a square with an unoccupied corner. The two players in possession take turns in playing the ball diagonally to the unoccupied corner, where it is intercepted by the third player. Using the same set-up, the player without a ball goes to get it and plays it to the corner he has just left

The players in possession carry out whichever movement they wish when they reach the defenders and a double movement halfway between two defenders

One pair receive balls from the other pair and beat their opponents at speed. Balls are then passed to the defenders from the other side and they become attackers

Physical condition

Two players pass the balls to the other side and cross over at speed to take the places of the players who have received them. Meanwhile, the latter have passed the balls and cross after them

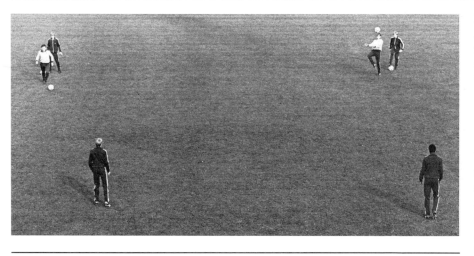

Left: The players in the foreground have passed the balls. The players in the background receive them and beat the players in the foreground. They then pass the balls back

Three players without a ball form a triangle. The three players in possession beat each of them twice by going round them on the outside. Roles constantly alternate, as does the direction in which the players go round the triangle

The player in possession beats his opponent or places a through pass for the supporting player. The defender receives the ball from the other side and the man without a ball becomes the supporting player

Right: The players in possession sprint with the ball to the opponent facing them. When they reach their opponents they shield the ball and sprint back with it. The players constantly switch roles

Four pairs form a large square. One player from each pair goes to collect the ball belonging to the next pair. He then goes round the square in the opposite direction, executing a movement as he goes past each opponent. When he reaches the place where he collected the ball he leaves it there and sprints back to his own place. The other four members of the pairs then do the same thing

Physical
condition

The players in light tops make long one-two combinations, then join the other group. After a certain number of minutes the players change roles and those in dark tops make combinations

Three pairs of players beat the permanent defenders in the middle in turn, either by dribbling or by passing

The players in possession work back and forth between two players. Again, all sorts of variations are possible. The players constantly switch roles

The players in dark shorts act alternately as defender and one-touch assistant. The players in white engage in individual play or make one-two combinations. Roles switch

Left: The players in possession beat their opponents, stop the ball, then take up position as defenders, whereupon the other players become attackers

The two players in white work in turns. They beat the defender, then come back and either beat him again or make a one-two combination with the other player

Physical condition

Two players in possession sprint in turns into an open space, encounter a defender and beat him

Two players take turns in beating a defender at speed. The defender operates on an imaginary line

Left: The two players in dark shorts must defend the imaginary line. After the attackers have made a given number of attempts to beat them, the roles change

Jump with one leg, land on the other, hop and jump as explosively as possible with the same leg

The same exercise, but now jump as far sideways as possible

Jump as explosively as possible with one leg, land on the other, bend the knee and again jump as high as possible using one leg. A variant is to perform the jump as a hop by landing on the jumping leg

Physical condition

In a zigzag pattern, a cross jump followed by a hop with one leg and then with the other

Jump as far as possible sideways, bend the knees, then jump with the other leg

In a zigzag pattern, a short run-up followed by a jump, setting off from each leg alternately, and a heading action

Explosive power

The football world has little experience of power training because, like the various kinds of condition training, it was taken over from other sports. Trainers who argue that power training is not necessary on the grounds that many top players have never had any forget that these players have natural power, whereas other players who would otherwise reach the top fail to do so because they lack power, and particularly power of the explosive kind. Pre-season power training sessions using modern equipment designed for that purpose can do no harm, and it is also very useful to have one session a week during the season. In this training plan explosive power is developed through the innumerable exercises in which explosive action is called for. It can be further developed by jumping, thus making use of your own body weight.

If a player makes twenty jumps, setting off ten times from his right leg and ten times from his left, this means that each leg has pushed the weight of his body into the air ten times. The increase in thrust in the two legs will become apparent fairly quickly and this will also improve his speed.

Up to the age of twelve the players already jump enough in practising heading technique. Between the ages of thirteen and sixteen their explosive power and athleticism can gradually be increased by means of special jumping exercises.

Kevin Keegan
The right attitude

Kevin Keegan was born with a bold heart and a reasonable right foot. Thousands of boys start with more but don't become captains of England and European Footballers of the Year before retiring at thirty-four as millionaires.

Keegan's achievement lay in extracting the utmost from himself. He is the prime example of what can be done with the right attitude.

He wasn't big so he worked with weights to build himself the rippling torso of a boxing champion. And he used his assets of courage, energy and intelligence to compensate for any defect of natural ability.

Courage in jumping against tall defenders made him a threat in the air. Energy to burn meant no defence dare leave him alone, and his quick brain saw the openings that others missed.

Keegan is the proof that a young player with the right outlook can go a long way – even if, as happened to Kevin, professional clubs reject him at first.

Phase 6 | Defensive qualities

The increase in defensive tactics and the development of players' defensive qualities are disturbing, and the more so because the development of attacking qualities in the players has not kept pace. You can read all about defensive concepts in the specialist literature, but nowhere, unfortunately, can you read how to learn attacking techniques. That is why this training plan is concerned almost entirely with attack. Naturally, attention work rate and mentality are constantly engaged in a fight for the ball. A technically gifted player has so much control over his body that he can defend in a much more correct way.

The advantage of this training plan is that players who have attacking qualities will want to demonstrate them during a game. A team which is technically strong wants to pin the opponents in their own half, at the same time taking measures to cope with counter-attacks. For a technically gifted team this is the best defence. When possession is lost, players of this kind immediately cover. Personalities detest running after an opponent. Permanent man-to-man marking is just as unrealistic as permanent zonal marking. If the defenders also have individual qualities that enable them to beat an opponent, man-to-man marking, except in the case of the

tion is also paid to defensive qualities. Defence has played a substantial part in all the competitive forms of practice and group games in the previous phases. You have already learned how to use your body correctly to shield the ball from an opponent when you receive a pass and come away with the ball and in all the exercises and games you have had to defend in a correct manner. The footballers who survive on the strength of

strikers, will play an increasingly smaller role. Once you have mastered all the attacking techniques, the group games provide all the opportunity you need to master zonal marking and the organization of a defence.

1. Sliding tackles

Sliding tackle with the outside of the foot, with and without an opponent. The other leg is to the side of the body

The sliding tackle is the only defensive technique we shall deal with. If it is carried out with technical perfection the danger of injury is nil for both the defender and the attacker. If you pin your opponents down in their own half it is reassuring to have mastered the sliding tackle because this enables you to play in a line.

There are six ways of carrying out a sliding tackle. The agility and suppleness acquired in the previous phases can be put to good use here. In practising sliding tackles it is advisable to wear 'sliding trousers' made of soft canvas to avoid grazing. Though attacking play is what really draws the crowds, a perfectly executed sliding tackle will do football no harm, because it is one of the many arts of the game.

Sliding tackle with the sole, with and without an opponent. The other leg is under the body

Sliding tackle with the inside of the foot, with and without an opponent, the ankle on the ground. The other leg is to the side of the body

Left: 'Sliding trousers' of soft canvas prevent grazing

Sliding tackle. Trap the ball with the inside of the foot, but now sideways

Sliding tackles

Sliding tackle, with and without opponent. Trap the ball with the inside of the foot. The other leg is bent under the body

Sliding tackle, with and without opponent. Kick the ball away. The other leg is bent under the body

Two pairs. The two players perform sliding tackles in which they kick the balls out of the demarcated area. A number of variants are possible. The other two players can play the balls back into the demarcated area or act as opponents

Peter Reid
The late developer

Recognition came late for Peter Reid of Everton. His twenty-ninth birthday was approaching when the Professional Footballers' Association voted him their 1985 Player of the Year. He is the first non-international to win the award.

Reid proves how older footballers can continue improving and developing by working on the techniques. It's only by acquiring greater agility and technical skill that attackers can prevail against modern defenders under orders to: 'Close 'em down!'

Reid is an example of how little working-space a creative player needs to disrupt a defence; although an infrequent scorer himself, he made many of the goals that took a revived Everton to Wembley and the top of the First Division.

He himself is a revival. Four years of major injuries – including a broken knee-cap and a broken leg with Bolton – slashed his transfer valuation from £600,000 to £60,000, which is all Everton paid for him.

For the money, they got a little man with a big brain who was prepared to slog away at regaining match-fitness and a lost yard of pace.

The lesson of Reid is: 'Never give up!'

Phase 7

Moving with and without the ball

The fashionable term 'collective play' has scarcely been used so far. Nonetheless, you have been working towards collective play from the very first training session, because without the techniques a player is powerless and for such players to play well collectively is impossible. You must be strong individually to play collectively. For years now the two have been placed in the reverse order, with predictable results. At the end of their careers footballers are still as limited technically as when they began.

If you learn all the techniques in youth you will have every opportunity of developing into a football personality. In the games with larger groups (five against five, seven against seven, attackers against defenders) the player must have a wide view of what is happening on the field; moving without the ball becomes important, because everyone knows that the ball determines the tempo. In practice, however, direct play is often impossible, par-

Three against three with two neutral one-touch assistants

Three against three with three neutral assistants between the posts. Players can score by dribbling the ball over the imaginary line

ticularly in and around the penalty area. Usually you have to get past an opponent to create a scoring opportunity; now that you have mastered the techniques for doing this you must make use of them. In addition, you must learn how and when to position yourself in such a way that the man with the ball has opportunities for passing.

The coaches will now have enough players capable of putting their ideas into practice, because all the players who have followed this training plan have command of attacking techniques. The positions for which the players are best suited will have become apparent in the course of their training. They must now receive specialized training for those positions. Despite the fact that they are primarily responsible for the team as a whole, the coaches too must continue to work on the players' individual development.

Four against four with two neutral assistants

Four against four with one neutral player. Players can score by dribbling the ball over the three imaginary lines. When a team has scored it retains possession and players try to score in the other two goals

Three against three with three neutral assistants

Moving with
and without the ball

Three against three with four neutral assistants

Three against three with one neutral player

Four against four with four assistants (the keepers)

Better to start young

Four players take turns in practising one-two combinations or beating their opponent and join the other group

Three players take turns in making one-two combinations or beating their opponent. The other two act alternately as defender and assistant

Women's football

The quality of women's football still leaves something to be desired, because most women start to play at a later age. Now that girls are starting to join football clubs at ever younger ages there are great possibilities for women's football, certainly in the technical sphere. The fact that women have less power and speed than men makes this training plan highly suitable for them, because they must concentrate on mastering the techniques. If a girl starts to follow the plan at the age of ten, within a few years she will be supple and strong on the ball.

Men often make derogatory remarks about women's football. What they forget is that, almost without exception, they themselves are limited and awkward in possession despite the fact that they have been members of a club for years. Women's football unquestionably has a future, particularly if the players concentrate on technically creative football.

More and more girls are taking up football at a young age

Practising the ball techniques

A new generation of footballers

I hope we agree by now that youngsters need a coach who can teach them the techniques of the top players. He must also give them the chance to use those techniques in order that they can develop into good players and rise above the ranks of the nondescript.

No training plan can ever be complete. If a coach, or player, works intensively on the techniques and exercises given here he will constantly discover or invent new ones and greater variety can be added.

Through club sessions and homework, after a while the players will begin to taste success. Once they do so, no further encouragement will be needed from the coach, because success acts like a drug on a footballer. The result will be a new generation of footballers, footballers who no longer wait for the trainer's whistle but practise of their own accord with the ball, think and talk about their development and work on it themselves. In this way they will acquire the individual, technically creative qualities which are indispensable attributes in an outstanding player.